MEMBERSHIP ROLES IN FIELD RESEARCH

PATRICIA A. ADLER
University of Colorado, Boulder
PETER ADLER
University of Denver

Qualitative Research Methods,
Volume 6

SAGE PUBLICATIONS
The Publishers of Professional Social Science
Newbury Park   Beverly Hills   London   New Delhi

For information address:

SAGE Publications, Inc.
2111 West Hillcrest Drive
Newbury Park, California 91320

SAGE Publications Inc.
275 South Beverly Drive
Beverly Hills
California 90212

SAGE Publications Ltd.
28 Banner Street
London EC1Y 8QE
England

SAGE PUBLICATIONS India Pvt. Ltd.
M-32 Market
Greater Kailash I
New Delhi 110 048 India

International Standard Book Number 0-8039-2760-6
0-8039-2578-6 (pbk.)

Library of Congress Catalog Card No. 86-61912

FIRST PRINTING

When citing a University Paper, please use the proper form. Remember to cite the correct
Sage University Paper series title and include the paper number. One of the following
formats can be adapted (depending on the style manual used):

(1) AGAR, MICHAEL H. (1985) Speaking of Ethnography. Sage University Paper
series on Quantitative Research Methods, Volume 2. Newbury Park, CA: Sage.

or

(2) Agar, Michael H. 1985. *Speaking of Ethnography.* Sage University Paper series on
Quantitative Research Methods (Vol. 2). Newbury Park, CA: Sage.

CONTENTS

To Jack and Stan—
one taught us how,
the other reminded us why

EDITORS' INTRODUCTION

Fieldwork is something of a peculiar idea. At heart, it refers to prolonged episodes during which lone researchers visit strange groups and insert themselves in the daily lives of the members. Fieldwork is not quite the same when it is organized as an expedition of many researchers or pursued as a short, sharp, and structured matter. There must be an almost hauntingly personal, deeply felt, emergent, and highly particularistic character for social research to count as authentic fieldwork. Patricia and Peter Adler explore these themes in this sixth contribution to the Qualitative Research Methods Series. Their attention is aimed at several forms of open-air fieldwork in sociology. Three ideal-type membership roles are used to depict historical and current fieldwork forms. The prescribed method requires, in all cases, being there; but each subtype of membership role is distinguished by the degree of fieldworker involvement in the affairs of the group studied. Curiously, the more attached, comfortable, and committed the researcher is within the group studied, the more it appears that fieldworkers and cultures may occasionally find and embrace one another for reasons that have little or nothing to do with the formal justification of the study. The social underpinnings of such a mutual attraction are covered in some detail in this monograph, as are the risks and rewards associated with the various membership roles. The wisdom put forth by the Adlers is akin to the "know thyself" command of Socrates. Fieldworkers unwilling or unable to sort out what is personally seductive or repulsive about potential research domains best beware. That fieldworkers are sometimes unnaturally resistent or blind to such private pulls and pushes is a point convincingly made in this monograph.

—John Van Maanen
Peter K. Manning
Marc L. Miller

PREFACE

This book, as much as possible, is written for both the novice and the professional field researcher. As such, we have tried to keep the prose jargon-free, while still orienting the text to the sophisticated reader who has grappled with some of these issues before. We have filled the book with relevant, contemporary examples to illustrate and define as well as possible the various experiences and roles we discuss. In this regard, we have made a conscientious effort, wherever possible, to select the most recent examples of field research, rather than relying on the same timeworn "classic" studies found in so many expositions of participant-observation methodology. In some cases we draw upon unpublished manuscripts still in the working stages. In these instances, we try to provide as much information for the reader as possible in the event he or she would like to further pursue this research. We have also drawn upon our own experiences as much as possible, especially our research on upper-level drug dealers and college athletes. In these cases, since first Patti and then Peter, respectively, were the principle investigators, we refer to ourselves in the first person. As in all our previous writings, though, we have shared equally in the writing and conceptualizing of this book.

Our hope is that *Membership Roles in Field Research,* along with the other volumes in this series, adds to the "revolution" currently taking place in qualitative methodology. For the first time in several decades, we are again, in the 1980s, addressing key issues in the discipline and questioning some of our preconceived notions about the epistemology of field research. The issues brought forth here, while perhaps controversial in part, are intended to "raise our consciousness" and make us more reflexive in doing our research. We hope that future researchers are intrigued by these questions.

Many people, both directly and indirectly, have helped make us aware of some of these issues. We have been profoundly and deeply affected by our relationships with Jack Douglas and Stanford Lyman, our two friends, colleagues, and mentors, to whom this book is dedicated. Jack, during our six years in San Diego, constantly reminded us about the subtle nuances and difficult travails that doing field research entails. He provided for us the lens through which we view the world. Stan, most especially during a glorious fall 1985 semester in Tulsa, reminded us about the power of sociological reasoning, the need to see people in their natural habitat, and the relationship between our ideas and the history of sociological thought. Burke Rochford, our colleague at the University of Tulsa, sat down with us for long hours explaining the more recent developments in ethnomethodology. Most critically, he made available to us his notes from Harold Garfinkel's seminar in ethnomethodology at the University of California, Los Angeles (hereafter referred to as Garfinkel, 1980), which crystalized our thinking about this particular branch of the theory. Herbert Gans and Jennifer Hunt provided particularly detailed and extensive comments on earlier drafts of this manuscript, pointing out errors of omission and commission, unclear points, and salient examples. Many others provided additional feedback, helpful comments, and critical information: David Altheide, Jean Blocker, Jay Corzine, Fred Davis, Burke Forrest, Myron Glazer, Ruth Horowitz, John Johnson, Peter Manning, James Marquart, John Van Maanen, Alan Peshkin, Murray Wax, and Juniper Wiley. We received considerable support from the Departments of Sociology at the University of Tulsa and Oklahoma State University. Mitch Allen, editor at Sage, pushed, cajoled, and badgered us to get the manuscript in on time. Reba Lee assiduously and meticulously typed the final manuscript.

For the controversies implied by our statements in the following pages, we will take the heat, but we hope our friends will help put out the fire by further refining qualitative methodology.

MEMBERSHIP ROLES IN FIELD RESEARCH

PATRICIA A. ADLER
University of Colorado, Boulder
PETER ADLER
University of Denver

1. THE HISTORY AND EPISTEMOLOGY OF FIELDWORK ROLES

In conducting field research, sociologists are often compelled to put aside their academic or other everyday life roles. In their place, researchers must assume social roles that fit into the worlds they are studying. Their perspectives on these worlds and the kinds of information they can learn about them are greatly influenced, however, by the character of the research roles they choose. In this volume, we consider the nature of field researchers' roles, the extent to which researchers can or should be integrated into the empirical settings they study, and the effect this has on the data they gather. Specifically, we focus on a range of roles that involve regular and intimate contact with members of the group being studied, where researchers participate as members in some or all of the group's everyday activities. Critical to these roles, which differentiates them from more observational forms of field research, is their *insider* affiliation; researchers do not interact with the group as detached outsiders (the "wallflower" approach), but instead take on *membership* status. For our purposes, we interpret research membership in the broadest sense, as comprising a continuum of roles ranging from the empathic but less involved participant who establishes a peripheral membership role within the group, to the fully committed convert or prior participant.

The Chicago School

When one thinks of the history of the field research tradition in sociology, the University of Chicago's department in the 1920s comes to mind. Under the auspices and guidance of Robert Park and Ernest Burgess, a number of classic studies were conducted that drew upon unsophisticated and often rudimentary techniques that served as the foundations for field research. During the 1980s, a renewed interest in these early years has arisen, and a debate has been generated over whether "participant observation" began during this early period or during a later era (Anderson, 1983; Bulmer, 1983, 1984; Cavan, 1983; Platt, 1983; Shalin, 1986; Thomas, 1983a). We will therefore differentiate in our discussion between the first and second generation of Chicago fieldworkers, tracing their influence on the development and style of field research.

Park and Burgess drew their theoretical inspiration from a variety of diverse sources. Park's background as a journalist oriented him toward naturalistic, empirical work, and his time employed by Booker T. Washington familiarized him with some anthropological writings on race (Park, 1915, 1950). Academically, he was influenced by the pragmatists, having studied with Cooley and Dewey at Michigan before he became a reporter (Park, 1973). Returning to his studies later, he worked with William James, Josiah Royce, George Santayana, and Hugo Munsterberg at Harvard, then traveled to Germany to study under Simmel, Windelband, and Knopp (Park, 1973). Upon his appointment to the faculty at the University of Chicago he was exposed to the interdisciplinary influence of John Watson (behaviorism) in neuropsychology, Edward Sapir in linguistic anthropology, George Herbert Mead in philosophy, and W. I. Thomas in his own department.

He and Burgess emphasized to their students the importance of using the city of Chicago as a laboratory to study human nature and society (Park, 1929). They urged them to seek the subjective point of view of the actor by abandoning the detached observation of the journalist and striving for empathy and an imaginative participation in the lives of others (Bulmer, 1984). The life history, or case study, approach was the primary means they used for penetrating this subjective sphere, which involved the use of mixed methods, including formal or depth interviews, informal interviews, casual conversation, observation, and the collection of historical archives, newspaper files, police and court records, and other documentary evidence (see Bulmer, 1984; Burgess, 1927). While it was not the vogue at the time to write explicitly about the methods used in conducting a particular study, enough information can now be gleaned to ascertain that Anderson's *The Hobo* (1923), Cressey's *The Taxi Dance Hall* (1932), Thrasher's *The Gang* (1927), and Landesco's *Organized Crime in Chicago* (1929), among others, involved the use of those naturalistic field methods that would later be defined more formally as *participant observation*. These include prior membership, participation in the group's activities, using covert roles, consciously attempting to penetrate fronts, cross-checking accounts, and generally hanging out (Anderson, 1975; Bulmer, 1984; Cressey, 1983; Landesco, 1925; Thrasher, 1928). Park and Burgess thus operated during a period when reflections on and codification of sociological methods were practically nonexistent, yet their strong natural instincts for data gathering led them to pioneer techniques that would lay the groundwork for a subsequent range of both qualitative and quantitative methodologies (Bulmer, 1984; Platt, 1981, 1983).

In the 1930s, the Department of Sociology at Chicago lost its national position of preeminence. Park had retired early in the decade and Burgess ceased to mentor many students (Cavan, 1983). Departments on the East and West Coasts began to rise in predominance, establishing the *American Sociological Review* as the major journal in the field. By the 1940s and 1950s, with the advent of Parsons's rise at Harvard and Columbia's growing dominance in the field of public opinion polling and survey research, sociology in America had shifted to a more quantitative paradigm. It was during this postwar period that the second generation of Chicago fieldworkers emerged to generate a new wave of empirical studies.

Several faculty members created an atmosphere that was sympathetic to field research, and both supported and guided students in doing field studies. Herbert Blumer, the principal advocate of symbolic interactionism, was sympathetic to fieldwork and worked with many students on empirical dissertations. Everett Hughes, who drew upon a more structural and situational theoretical perspective, was perhaps the strongest driving force behind the development of participant observation as a distinct methodology, and encouraged many students to study occupational cultures (Gans, 1985). A third senior faculty member working with students on field studies was William Lloyd Warner, who had completed the classic Yankee City studies with P. S. Lunt (Warner and Lunt, 1941, 1942). Two younger faculty members, Anselm Strauss and David Riesman, were also instrumental in encouraging and sponsoring participant observation fieldwork. The faculty during this era was more fragmented than during the time of Park and Burgess, and was seen by many insiders as not constituting a "school" at all (Gans, 1985; Riesman, 1983; Wax, 1986).[1] In fact, just as each of these faculty members advocated their own eclectic perspective, their graduate students also concocted unique blends of theory and epistemology. Yet despite the creativity characterizing these fieldworkers, part of the task of understanding their contributions and legacy lies in identifying the main streams and patterns underlying their collective approach. In so doing, we do not mean to stereotype or oversimplify, but rather to cull the most enduring and significant commonalities unifying this major academic movement. Thus, the overall atmosphere that pervaded the department encouraged students to conduct empirical studies "from the inside" (Adler and Adler, 1980) and to develop theoretical concepts out of their research (Davis, 1986). Classic works that came out of this era include Becker, Geer, and Hughes, *Making the Grade* (1968); Becker, Geer, Hughes, and Strauss, *Boys in White* (1961); Becker, *Outsiders* (1963); Davis, *Passage Through Crisis* (1963); Gold, *The Chicago Flat Janitor* (1950); Gusfield, *Symbolic Crusade* (1963); Goffman, *The Presentation of Self in Everyday Life* (1959); Habenstein, *The American Funeral Director* (1954); Roth, *Timetables* (1963); and Stone, *Clothing and Social Relations* (1959).

Methodologically, the most significant contribution of this era lay in the development and codification of the technique of participant observation.[2] Wax (1971) argues that the dominance of statistical techniques both inside and outside the department, and their proponents' vocal claims that theirs was the "scientific sociology," impelled the Chicago fieldworkers to scrutinize, explain, and justify their research procedures. Thus not only did their monographs begin to carry the now standard methods appendixes or chapters but a variety of articles, then monographs, and finally sets of readings appeared that explicitly discussed the principles, practices, and problems of participant observation (see Becker, 1967; Becker and Geer, 1960; Gold, 1958; Junker, 1960; McCall and Simmons, 1969; Miller, 1952; Schwartz and Schwartz, 1955; Vidich, 1955). The thrust of participant observation was distinct from the earlier life history/case study approach in its abandonment of those techniques associated with the greater extremes of subjectivity and objectivity. Quantitative and statistical techniques had been developed and refined by Lazarsfeld, Merton, Stouffer, and others, so fieldworkers abandoned them. They left the use of personal documents, letters, diaries, and other written materials primarily to those pursuing the historical method. They broadened their focus, however, from the individual case to the community, subculture, or social movement. In so doing, they drew on the anthropological model (Wax, 1971), which came to Hughes, in part, through the influence of his closest colleague and friend at Chicago, Robert Redfield (an anthropologist and the son-in-law of Robert Park). Hughes believed that the bifurcation of sociology and anthropology (on both a disciplinary and a departmental level) led to the dehydration of sociology (Riesman, 1983). He therefore advocated that researchers participate personally in the activities and social worlds of their subjects (Radcliffe-Brown, 1958), yet at the same time maintain some objectivity and detachment in their role and analysis (to a greater extent than the first generation Chicagoans).

The participant observation fieldwork conducted and codified by this second generation of Chicagoans has persisted in influence to the present day. Most of the current fieldwork texts present the practice and philosophy advocated by these individuals, and it has come to stand as the "classical," or "Chicago School" tradition in field research. Yet, ironically, when most people talk or think about the Chicago School they visualize the 1920s-1930s era (see Bulmer, 1984; Thomas, 1983b). While the work of the first generation of Chicago field researchers clearly anticipates and lays the groundwork for the types of mainstream fieldwork practiced in the 1980s, it is the reformulation of Chicago School epistemology that began in the 1940s (when its members questioned whether they should be considered a "school" at all), and that continues to the present, that actually constitutes this tradition. It is the methodology forged and codified by this second generation of Chicago field researchers that has emerged as the heritage of the Chicago School.

A primary belief of the Chicago School of field research is the view that its goal is to contribute to general theoretical statements about cultural and social life (Emerson, 1983: 19). Unlike the more structural or quantitative sociologies that dominate the mainstream of American sociology, its practitioners argue that the best way to gain an understanding of the social world is to study the perspectives of the members themselves (Blumer, 1962, 1969; Schutz, 1962, 1967). In order to do this they consider it necessary to venture, firsthand, into the places where the activities that interest them are taking place, and to observe human group life "*in situ*" (Hughes, 1971). Only by interacting directly and "naturalistically" (Denzin, 1970; Schatzman and Strauss, 1973) with the people they are interested in studying can sociologists come to understand fully both the mundane details and the pivotal concerns of their subjects' lives (Becker, 1963; Polsky, 1969). Only by observing their subjects' everyday affairs unfolding and by talking with them about specific events as they are occurring can sociologists discover the way "natives" interpret and ascribe meaning to their complex and manifold activities. Only by participating intensively and continuously with the poeple they want to study can sociologists attain the intuitive empathy necessary to grasp their subjects' perspectives on the social world. The term *Chicago School* refers to researchers' ability to know and understand the broad range of social meanings by which members of a social scene organize their attitudes, behavior, and, ultimately, their social world as *verstehen,* a process of interpretive understanding.

In order to acquire valid data about research subjects, fieldworkers have to gain their confidence. Chicago School researchers believe that this is a fairly nonproblematic enterprise, considering people generally straightforward, honest, and cooperative (Blumer, 1969; Gold, 1958; Junker, 1960; Palmer, 1928). Taking a humanistic approach to human behavior, they believe that "rapport could be achieved by anyone who is a good and humane human being" (Freilich, 1970: 540). Perhaps Peshkin (1984: 257) best sums up this point, as he expressed his initial beliefs upon entering the field:

> If researchers appear good, honest, and decent, then they are rewarded with trust. If trusted, they have the open sesame to meetings, documents, interviews, etc.

Field researchers, then, should enter their settings, announce their intentions, and begin to interact with the people they encounter. Traditionally, their initial activities are unfocused and merely involve "hanging out" (Becker and Geer, 1960; Hughes, 1971; Liebow, 1967; Whyte, 1955). Eventually, they build up to asking, "What is going on?" Researchers should let members of the setting gradually get to know them as they hang around in this manner, so that people realize the nonthreatening nature of their research intentions (Becker, 1963) and their overall interest and sincerity. Johnson (1975) refers to this as the "individual-morality" premise of developing trust, where researchers seek to achieve their subjects' confidence by presenting themselves as conscientious and likable individuals ("nice guys").

Members of the Chicago School have proposed a variety of roles researchers can adopt in the field. The most widely known of these are the complete observer, observer-as-participant, participant-as-observer, and complete participant (Gold, 1958; Junker, 1960), ranging from least to most involved in the group and its activities. The observer-as-participant is a rather detached, overt role, typically involving brief and highly formalized interaction between researchers and members, with no attempts to establish enduring relationships by either side. The participant-as-observer is also an overt role, but involves greater contact and intimacy between researchers and their subjects. Fieldworkers generally form a series of relationships with setting members in which select natives become respondents and key informants, helping researchers gain further insight and entrée into the setting. Observers-as-participants usually move through several stages of involvement with setting members. Eventually, if things go well, they may attain a more insider status from which they can better gather data. These stage evolutions are accompanied by revised role definitions; members gradually loosen the role they had initially cast onto researchers and let a new role emerge that incorporates the way researchers and members want to be treated by each other. The progressive evolution of stages may also reflect researchers' increasing acceptance by the group, so that their role shifts from a provisional (marginal) to a categorical (involved) membership status. This type of research role was the one most commonly advocated by second-generation Chicago School field researchers. Finally, in the role of complete participant, researchers operate secretly and feign conversion to membership in the group. This usually involves a process of induction and displays of commitment, and such researchers must manage the often conflicting role expectations of their "real" (sociological) and pretended (member) selves. The complete participant may develop a heightened sense of self-awareness due to having to walk a tightrope between his or her disguised self and his or her hidden, observing self.

Within these typologies, Chicago School sociologists recognize the existence of two distinct research strategies: the *overt* role, where sociologists openly admit to members that they are conducting a study, and the *covert* role, where sociologists do not admit the research dimensions of their participation. These strategies generally have been portrayed as mutually exclusive; researchers are encouraged to choose either one or the other, but not both. The dangers of trying to play both roles in the same setting are evident: Researchers have to worry constantly about the existence and possible convergence of their multiple identities and "cover stories." Thus the Chicago School generally discourages researchers from using both roles simultaneously. In fact, they overwhelmingly oppose the covert role altogether for the following reasons: (1) It poses practical problems when researchers want to discover information or attitudes they would not ordinarily learn as mere participants; (2) its deceptive nature poses ethical questions; and (3) it involves researchers too deeply in the members' perspective and can lead to problems of "going native" (which we will discuss shortly) (Bulmer, 1980; Cassell, 1980; Cassell and Wax, 1980;

Erikson, 1967; Reiman, 1979; Warwick, 1974). Thus most Chicago School research has been conducted using the overt role, with participants fully aware of sociologists' identities (Gold, 1958; Hammersley and Atkinson, 1983; Junker, 1960; Lofland, 1971; Schatzman and Strauss, 1973).

Field roles, for the Chicago School researchers, are fluid and changing. Rather than adopting one role and keeping it for the duration of their study, sociologists often progress through different roles over the course of gathering data (Denzin, 1970; Hammersley and Atkinson, 1983; Janes, 1961; Oleson and Whittaker, 1967). For instance, individuals might enter a setting as passive participants, watching others from a safe and reclusive vantage point, while saying little. After getting to know a few members and getting the "lay of the land," they may shift roles and begin interacting with members as moderate participants. From there, some researchers further increase their involvement with individuals, the group, and/or the organization to an active or complete level, while others remain moderate participants (or are blocked from achieving any greater form of participation). In other cases, researchers may jump right into the setting in an active participatory role, only to increase, diminish, or hold their involvement constant thereafter. Researchers' roles may thus shift and evolve throughout their studies (see Spradley, 1980). Complicating this is the fact that researchers may occasionally become involved in playing several roles simultaneously with different research audiences (Burgess, 1982; Denzin, 1970).

The type of role researchers take in their settings is a function of four factors (Junker, 1960). First, there are always conditions inherent in the setting that exist prior to the fieldworkers' arrival that may affect their getting in, staying in, or easing out of the scene. This can include the degree of secrecy involved in the setting, participants' modes of relating to outsiders, and the participants' contact with other researchers. This is particularly true of sociologists who study deviant groups. Due to the obvious need for secrecy and self-protection among people who violate laws and mores, sociologists trying to penetrate into their midst may assume that they will not be allowed too much access to insiders' secrets (see, especially, Becker, 1963; Carey, 1972; Douglas, 1972; Polsky, 1969).

Second, fieldworkers' abilities, identities, theoretical orientations, self-understandings, reference-group attachments, demographic characteristics, or any number of personal factors may influence the roles they seek or attain. This involves such factors as researchers' prior knowledge of or involvement with the setting or setting members, their degree of comfort with the people and activities practiced in the setting, and their methodological beliefs about becoming too closely involved with the setting on a personal basis. For instance, in Peshkin's (1986) study of a fundamentalist Christian school, a combination of his personal biography (he was a Jew), his personal beliefs (he did not agree with the absolutist nature of the members' values or life-style), and his moral convictions (he could neither convert nor pretend to do so), precluded his participating fully as a member of the group.

Third, field researchers' roles may be affected by changes in the setting itself during the research period. These may be structural changes in the group or even changes brought about by the presence of the researcher. For example, in our study of college athletes (Adler, 1984; Adler and Adler, 1985, forthcoming), Peter was cast into the role of "team sociologist." In this guise, he was expected to advise, counsel, and guide players about their academic careers, relations with the media, social lives, postcollege careers, and a host of other personal topics. Through this, he changed the way some of the players thought about the setting and affected the way they behaved. This, then, had the effect of changing his role, as they came to him with their problems and he became more of a participant and less of an observer.

Finally, researchers, themselves, may undergo changes, organically, as people, as role-players, or as social scientists, and therefore seek out new roles for collecting data within the setting. In Wax's study of Japanese-American relocation centers during the second world war, for example, she was hired to enter the camps as a participant observer and to record detailed accounts of what the Japanese-Americans were doing and saying (Wax, 1971: 63). Hers was to be a neutral and scholarly role. However, the intense political focus of the project as a whole led to the development of bitter factionalization in the camps, into which Wax was drawn. After a series of frustrating and upsetting events, Wax registered a formal protest with the Department of Justice. Shortly afterward, she was expelled from the setting. In reflecting on her role transformation, she notes that her behavior and attitudes, in participating in the struggle, came to resemble those of "a fighter in a resistance movement" (Wax, 1971: 174).

As a natural consequence of participating in their settings, sociologists may feel a pull toward even greater inclusion and involvement with their research subjects (Bogdan and Taylor, 1975; Gans, 1982b; Hammersley and Atkinson, 1983; Pollner and Emerson, 1983). Pressures, by members, to involve field researchers in their group can be categorized into three types of overtures (Pollner and Emerson, 1983: 237-243). First, members may make efforts to induct researchers as workers and situational resources in dealing with various instrumental tasks. This ranges from innocuous and unspecialized activities, such as serving as "go-fers," to more critical and central operations, such as mobilizing a part of the group for action or engaging in illegal activities on their behalf. For instance, Corsino (1984), in his study of political campaigns, frequently did the "grunt work" of the campaign: stuffing envelopes, serving as a delivery boy, clipping newspaper articles, and so on. While studying drug dealers and smugglers (see Adler, 1985), we encountered more serious requests for involvement and aid. At times we had to loan respondents money, testify in court on their behalf, allow them to conduct drug deals in our house, watch their children for extended periods of time, house them for several months when they were destitute, and several other dangerous activities. Sociologists who refuse such induction efforts, whether serious or mundane, may endanger their rapport with participants. Second, groups often try to induce fieldworkers into full membership, regarding them as potential recruits. Those groups who most freely welcome outsiders often have a hidden agenda to their ease of entry: they seek to convert the researcher to their beliefs. In these cases, induction attempts may be recurrent and firmly pressed. For example, in Rochford's (1985) study of Hare Krishnas, he was an open and constant target for possible conversion. Third, research subjects may seek to establish greater intimacy than sociologists desire. This can include attempted incursions into researchers' personal lives, family lives, sexual lives, and financial lives. This seems particularly to be the case for women fieldworkers. They report how men often "come on to them," trying to gain sexual favors in exchange for interviews, insights, opinions, or ideas. This kind of sexual "hustle," if either accepted or denied, can have serious ramifications for future data collection (see Easterday et al., 1977; Golde, 1970; Warren and Rasmussen, 1977; Wax, 1979, for further discussions of these issues).

Pulls toward greater involvement do not always stem from the research subjects, however, but may originate even more strongly from within fieldworkers. As Gans (1982b: 54) notes:

> I had to fight the urge to shed the emotional handcuffs that bind the researcher, and to react simultaneously to the situation, to relate to people as a person and to derive pleasure rather than data from the situation.

Inner urges toward involvement may be prompted not only by researchers' concerns about events in the setting but by their feelings of unnaturalness in the detached participant observer role. For instance, in our study of college athletes (Adler, 1984), Peter never felt comfortable just "hanging around," although the head coach originally accepted this as his research role. In order to feel fully at ease, he created for himself the official position of Academic Advisor. This gave him a more clearly defined role in the setting and permitted him to offer the team something in exchange for the data he was gathering. In addition, researchers may just feel more comfortable in a setting when their data-gathering role closely approximates the spontaneity and involvement of their everyday life behavior (see Corsino, 1984). These pressures have the effect of drawing researchers toward taking membership roles in their settings.

Generally, Chicago School field researchers do not condone this pull toward overinvolvement. Instead, they seek to balance this by remaining "objective" and "detached" (Becker and Geer, 1960; Blumer, 1969; Burgess, 1982; Gans, 1982a; Gold, 1958; Hammersley and Atkinson, 1983; Junker, 1960; Lofland, 1971; Pollner and Emerson, 1983; Schatzman and Strauss, 1973). As Shalin (1986: 21) expresses it:

> The sociologist qua participant observer never submerges himself entirely in the community life he studies; he measures his involvement with detachment, sympathy with reflection, heart with reason.

Overinvolvement has been most often conceptualized as the problem of "going native." Defined in a broad sense, going native brings specific dangers to the research and researcher that must be avoided. First, going native involves developing an overrapport with the research subjects that could harm the data-gathering process. Becoming too closely aligned with one group in the setting may prevent the researcher from gaining access to the perspectives of other groups in the scene (Bogdan and Taylor, 1975; Hammersley and Atkinson, 1983; Miller, 1952; Stein, 1964). Overrapport may also bias researchers' own perspectives, leading them to accept uncritically the views of the members (or one group of members) as their own (Gold, 1958; Hammersley and Atkinson, 1983; Miller, 1952; Willis, 1977). The greatest danger in going native occurs when researchers completely lose their analytical perspective. This point is argued by Hammersley and Atkinson (1983: 102):

> There can be no question of total commitment, "surrender," or "becoming." There must always remain some part held back, some social and intellectual "distance." For it is in the "space" created by this distance that the analytic work of the ethnographer gets done. Without that distance, without such analytic space, the ethnography can be little more than the autobiographical account of a personal conversion.

Further, by becoming overly involved as participants in their research settings, fieldworkers risk influencing the phenomena they seek to study. The Chicago School therefore takes the objectivist view that field researchers should strive to exert no influence at all on their research subjects.

Finally, Chicago School sociologists also caution researchers that their selves, as their major research instrument, may be fundamentally affected and changed by overinvolvement with research subjects. By abandoning their attachment to scientific objectivity and their commitment to social science, they open themselves to the full strength of emotional forces affecting setting members. In its most extreme form, the change in researchers' selves may result in their transferring their identity and loyalty to the setting, totally abandoning the task of analysis and failing to return from the field.

To avoid these common pitfalls, sociologists have developed techniques to diminish the extent of their involvement with the people they study. Pollner and Emerson (1983) have identified four major processes sociologists employ (not always successfully) to limit the extent of their role in the setting and to keep themselves from becoming further drawn in over the course of their research. First, researchers employ preemptive moves designed to deter members from attempting to overly involve them in the setting. For example, researchers may differentiate themselves demographically from their respondents, feign a novice or ignorant status over extended periods of time ("playing the boob"; Douglas, 1976), use physical positioning to situate themselves on the periphery of the action, and communicate distance and detachment through their body language. Horowitz (1986), in her study of Chicano gangs, felt it necessary to differentiate herself from the "chicks" who hung around the male gang members lest she become a target for sexual advances. Thus she chose not to dress like or use the idioms of the local gang girls.

Second, when confronted with members' explicit overtures to include them, researchers can directly decline these invitations or suggestions. Researchers may explicitly declare their unwillingness to participate in the scene more fully, but they risk the estrangement that may result from such a direct refusal. These refusals very often generate feelings of strain and alienation between the researcher and members. At one point during Corsino's (1984) study, for instance, he refused a direct request to scrub floors and to help prepare someone's home for a fund-raising reception, thinking he could gather more valuable data by observing the organizational preparations for the event. He notes the members' responses:

> The reactions of the campaign manager and volunteer director were more antagonistic than I expected. Over the next several days, I noticed a polite but unmistakable cooling in my relationship with these officials. . . . I began to feel more and more like an ingrate. . . . This, in turn, resulted in a rather barren period of fieldwork observations. . . . At best, I had become a passive observer [Corsino, 1984: 19-20].

Third, researchers can respond to members' efforts to involve them by indirectly evading, deflecting, or using tactfully vague responses to excuse themselves from greater commitment. This is especially common in factionalized settings where researchers are asked to ally themselves with one group, or in situations where a direct refusal could be taken as an insult. In these cases, researchers may subtly deliver negative messages by simply failing to act on the invitations of members. This tactic saved Golde (1970: 85) embarrassment on several occasions when she refused the amorous advances of the Mexican men she studied by feigning that she had not noticed or correctly interpreted their opening moves:

> It was often presented so tentatively, so indirectly, that I could pretend I didn't understand and he could pretend he hadn't really said anything, and both our feelings were saved.

Finally, researchers sometimes handle unavoidable individual or structural demands for commitment by ostensibly involving themselves, while secretly remaining detached. That is, they may speak and act as if they hold the values, beliefs, and philosophies of members, while subjectively reminding themselves of their different inner ideas and concerns. Peshkin (1984: 258-259) sums this up:

I manipulated my behavior, blending in like a chameleon when invisibility was in order and appearing in this or that posture when I needed to produce a particular effect. . . . Yet, since the human participant observer was always present, I was bothered by the arrogance of their belief that failing to adopt their Truth placed me in eternal jeopardy. As the proselytizing continued, I became more annoyed, at least the *private* "I" did [emphasis added].

The danger of this role pretense is that researchers may find themselves "psychologically engulfed" by their participation and develop inner impulses to involve and commit themselves more deeply.

The Chicago School thus advocates a fairly specific range of research roles for which, given the situational and structural contingencies of their settings, researchers should aim. By following this counsel and seeking to strike the appropriate levels, Chicago researchers, in effect, strive for *marginal* roles in their field settings (see Freilich, 1970). They want to observe the essence of ongoing activity while inconspicuously fading into the background. They want people to reveal to them intimate details of their attitudes, motivations, and feelings, without contributing the same in return. They want to poise themselves, intellectually, between "familiarity" and "strangeness" (Powdermaker, 1966), and socially, between being a "stranger" and a "friend" (Everhart, 1977). Only through this simultaneous insider-outsider position can they attain "creative insight" (Lofland, 1971). In sum, they aspire to the position of "marginal native" (Freilich, 1970) in whatever roles they take (Bogdan and Taylor, 1975; Bruyn, 1966; Burgess, 1982; Gans, 1968; Hammersley and Atkinson, 1983; Hughes, 1960; Jarvie, 1969; Junker, 1960; Paul, 1953; Pollner and Emerson, 1983; Powdermaker, 1966; Trice, 1956; Vidich, 1955; Williams, 1967).

Some Chicago School sociologists have taken an even more extreme position on marginality. They suggest that people who are drawn to participant observation fieldwork are chronically marginal types who naturally fall into peripheral social roles. As Gans (1982b: 61) suggests:

My hunch is that fieldwork attracts a person who, in Everett Hughes's words, "is alienated from his own background," who is not entirely comfortable in his new roles, or who is otherwise detached from his own society; the individual who is more comfortable as an observer than as a participant.

This may be the case when, as Burgess (1982: 1) remarks, researchers maintain membership in the culture where they were reared, while concomitantly establishing membership in the group they are studying. Rather than becoming a well-integrated member of two social worlds, one becomes "a sort of double marginal man, alienated from both worlds" (Evans-Pritchard, 1973: 3).

A word of caution must be added to conclude this discussion. These prescriptions and proscriptions are somewhat ideal typical in character.

While fieldworkers may initiate their research endeavor with the intention of pursuing the suggested role, their experience may cause them to stray from these initial aspirations. As Gans (1985) notes, "The method makes a shambles of logical positivism, and detachment goes by the board quickly during fieldwork." This is partly due to the situational contingencies researchers encounter and partly due, as Wax (1971: 41) notes, to the transformative effect of personally conducting a depth field investigation. The participant observer role thus has been broader and more adaptable in its practice than in its formal epistemology.

More Radical Views on Membership:
The California Sociologies of Everyday Life

The philosophical and sociological traditions of German idealism, phenomenology, interpretive sociology, and pragmatism were responsible for spawning both the participant observation epistemology and the loosely connected symbolic interactionist perspective at the University of Chicago.[3] More recently, a new generation of sociologists concerned with studying everyday life in the social world have continued to work within and expand these traditions. Existential sociologists and ethnomethodologists, among these, have been critical of both symbolic interactionism and the epistemological tenets of the Chicago School of fieldwork. Their critiques and subsequent beliefs have profound ramifications for researchers' roles in the field.

EXISTENTIAL SOCIOLOGY: THE INVESTIGATIVE PARADIGM

Existential sociology is located within a philosophical tradition that dates back to the ancient Greek culture. Early Greek existentialists include Thrasymachus, the Sophist from Chalcedon, who rejected Socrates' rational search for an understanding of human beings within the cosmos, and the god Dionysus, who represented the inner feelings and situated expressions of human beings, unbridled by any rational restrictions. More recently and directly, it draws on the existential philosophy of Martin Heidegger, Jean-Paul Sartre, and Maurice Merleau-Ponty, the phenomenology of Edmund Husserl, and the hermeneutics of Wilhelm Dilthey (Fontana, 1980).

Existential sociology differs from symbolic interactionism and other sociologies in its view of human beings as not merely rational, symbolic, or determined by the norms, values, classes, or social structure framing their existence. Instead, its proponents believe that people have strong elements of emotionality and irrationality, and often act on the basis of their situated feelings or moods. They are thus simultaneously both determined and free, affected by structural constraints while still mutable, changeable, and emergent (Zurcher, 1977). At the same time, society is complex and pluralistic, divided by power struggles among different groups. Torn by the loyalties of their different memberships, people experience inner conflict.

Since most groups in the society have things they want to hide from other groups, people present fronts to nonmembers. This creates two sets of realities about their activities: one presented to outsiders, and the other reserved for insiders. Drawing on the perspectives of Erving Goffman (1959) and Niccolo Machiavelli (1970), existentialists also believe that people manage the impressions they give off to others. Researchers, then, must penetrate these fronts to find out about human nature and human society (Douglas and Johnson, 1977).

This view of society has profound ramifications for existentialists' methodology. The only way to penetrate people's individual and group fronts is to become an insider, thereby gaining deep and direct personal experience in their worlds. Fieldworkers should establish friendly and trusting relations with members to maximize their access to insiders' position and information. They should then draw on their observations, experiences, and feelings as primary sources of data. Borrowing from the techniques of investigative journalists, existentialists cultivate key informants who can offer them insights and accounts. As these data are being collected, researchers should employ rigorous methodological strategies to ensure the validity of these accounts, cross-checking them against common sense, their own observations, the accounts of others, and hard facts whenever possible (Douglas, 1976).

Existentialists' conflictful image of society also leads them to advocate a mixed strategy of investigation. At times, in contrast to the Chicago School, researchers may be open and obvious (overt) with some members and secretive and obscure (covert) with others. We, for example, pursued a combination of overt and covert roles simultaneously in our study of drug dealers (Adler, 1985). Because of the secretive nature of the activity and the highly suspicious nature of the traffickers, we could not let everyone in the scene know we were conducting a study. To do so would have meant getting closed out to a large group of members. We therefore told some people about our research, but studied others secretly. The price we paid, however, included a constant concern that someone would "blow our cover," thereby risking the entire research project (if not our lives).

While a mixture of overt and covert roles can be undertaken by a single individual who relates in different ways to other individuals or groups within the setting, it is preferable to use two or more researchers working together as a team. Here, team members adopt different roles in the setting and place themselves with different key informants, thereby achieving a multiperspectival view of the scene (Douglas, 1976). This strategy can be especially enhanced when researchers complement each other in age and gender and can more easily get close to different groups in the setting (Warren and Rasmussen, 1977).

Team field research can be done in several ways. One of the most common is to organize a group of sociologists (usually a professor and a team of graduate students) to penetrate various aspects of the scene. For instance, in Douglas and Rasmussen's (1977) study of a nude beach, the two authors could only get first-hand data on male participants. Thus they used one sociologist who had informal relations with the police in the area to study the police officers' view, another graduate student who knew police officials to get the institutional view, some undergraduates to study the landowners, and, most important, a woman researcher to get the female perspective that was systematically closed to the two primary investigators. A second approach is for sociologists to join together with an established (or recently "retired") member of the setting. For instance, in Prus and Sharper's (1977) study of card and dice hustlers, Prus (the sociologist) joined with Sharper (a former hustler) to conduct interviews and corroborate data. Through Sharper's previous involvement in the scene, they were able to interview 40 professional hustlers who would not have been accessible to the sociologist alone. A third approach is for two (or more) sociologists, who are interested in disparate concepts within a same setting, to work together. Since negotiating entrée is often the most difficult task in conducting fieldwork, it may be beneficial to do this with someone else. Here, team members can both enhance the project's legitimacy and buoy each other during the initial stages of data gathering. For example, Kotarba (1983) and we (see Adler, 1981) teamed together to study the same professional athletic team, although we were interested in pain and momentum, respectively.

Johnson (1975: 86-90) suggests that mixed strategies may also be used to gain the trust of respondents. In his study of a state social work agency, he cites four features of his relationships with members that helped him to develop their trust. First, he employed the exchange approach, offering favors and assistance to setting members in exchange for research information (see also Wax, 1952). Second, he used the "individual-morality" approach, convincing respondents of his integrity and the nonthreatening nature of his research (the classical model). Third, he adopted a "membership morality," displaying the orientation of and commitment to the setting and its members. Last, he tried to fill members' psychological needs, being there when they needed someone to talk to, bounce ideas off, or keep them company. Basically, however, existential sociologists suggest that researchers have a wide latitude to select and combine appropriate strategies for developing members' trust. As long as researchers are cognizant of both public laws (particularly laws of privacy and confidentiality) and informal norms (rules of etiquette), they can follow their own moral prescriptions in conducting studies.

Upon entering the field, researchers should seek to experience the setting as much as possible like any new participant. This allows them to become socialized to the setting, to learn the taken-for-granted assumptions, to grasp the setting as insiders do and, as much as possible, to feel the way insiders feel. For instance, in our study of college athletes, by progressively gaining a membership role on the basketball team, Peter was able to experience personally the sudden impact of high pressure and media celebrity. He was also able to relate on an insider basis to freshman players who were cyclically thrust into the maelstrom of the season. Yet due to his lack of prior familiarity with this scene, he was able to recognize many features of the players' and coaches' perspectives that were influenced by the structural factors framing their experience. For this reason, existential sociologists argue that it is better for researchers to study settings with which they are not already familiar. By being familiar with their settings before they adopt the research perspective, they may lose the opportunity to see some of its important analytical features (Douglas, 1976).

This is not meant to denigrate the work of those researchers who are already members of the setting at the inception of their study. In fact, if one can defocus and desensitize oneself enough to do research, the previously attained membership role offers many clear advantages. For instance, in Kotarba's (1983) study of chronic pain sufferers, he was, to a large degree, aided by his own chronic back condition. Without this unfortunate situation, he never would have been able to feel the world as the members do. Thus lack of prior membership in the scene is an ideal, although not a necessary, aspect of the researcher-setting relationship.

Through their emphasis on depth, insider involvement, existential sociologists rebut the Chicago School's concern with going native for several reasons. First, they reject the claim that overfamiliarity leads researchers to assume the self-deceptions of the members. Self-deception is not caused by involvement per se, but by deep-rooted emotional conflicts within individuals. One way researchers can sidestep these problems is to avoid studying settings where they have preexisting emotional conflicts or moral judgments. For instance, when we moved to Oklahoma, a Bible Belt state, we were intrigued by the fundamentalist religious and teaching institutions that are so popular in the area. Although it piqued our sociological curiosity, we knew that our preconceived biases and emotional revulsion about such groups precluded our ever studying these organizations.

According to the classical perspective, another problem associated with going native is that researchers may assume the "natural attitude" (Schutz, 1962) of members. This refers to researchers' tendencies, arising from their overinvolvement, to take their settings' ongoing activities and meanings for granted. When this happens, they may fail to recognize adequately the theoretical significance of these events. As we have seen before, this is more associated with prior membership than with converted membership, but it calls into question the essence of researchers' work in the field. Scientific analysis does not occur within the realm of objective detachment (Peshkin, 1985; Reinharz, 1979). Rather, it falls within researchers' "theoretical stance" (Douglas, 1970), or sociological perspective, where they periodically withdraw from the everyday life actors' natural stance and engage in analytical self-reflection. Self-reflection is not enhanced by objective detachment, but is a trait that occurs naturally in some people and that can be cultivated by others.

In lieu of the problems cited by the Chicago School, existential sociologists' fear of overinvolvement is that, when researchers go native, they may fail to return from the field. Existential sociologists feel strongly that throughout their research, fieldworkers must maintain a commitment to remaining social scientists, eventually returning to the academic world to write their descriptions, observations, and analyses of their settings. The danger of overinvolvement thus lies in the seduction of the setting, enticing sociologists to transfer their allegiance elsewhere. For instance, in Forrest's (forthcoming) comparative study of spiritualist churches in England and California, it took her almost seven years before she was able to remove herself enough from her loyalties to members of these groups to write about them. She experienced inner conflicts due to the guilt she anticipated feeling should her manuscript hurt members' feelings, expose them to any kind of shame, or reveal to them that she did not always believe everything that she had pretended to believe. To some extent, all fieldworkers feel the "agony of betrayal" (Lofland, 1971) once they plumb respondents for their deepest emotions and beliefs, then leave the field to analyze these perspectives from a theoretical, detached framework.

Existential sociologists do not specifically advocate that fieldworkers become members of their settings in conducting research. Some settings demand that researchers become members in order to gain entrée. In these cases, researchers should become members if they feel they can. Existential sociologists do argue forcefully, however, for the necessity of obtaining an insider's perspective. To acquire this, they suggest that researchers form close relationships with key informants to gain uncensored and depth accounts. They should use their relationships with other members to supplement, cross-check, and interpret these accounts, further checking these accounts against hard evidence. Finally, they should add to all these the direct personal experience necessary to gain depth, subjective understanding of their everyday social reality.

The existential perspective thus breaks with the classical epistemology in rejecting the latter's assumption of a cooperative social world and cooperative research subjects. These are the result of the consensual postwar society during which time the participant observation methodology was forged. Existential sociology presents a more complex and concealed portrait of social settings and the members who populate them, urging researchers to collect their data in more investigative and multiperspectival ways. Finally, it legitimates researchers' own subjective experiences as an important source of data. Thus, ironically, the methods of existential sociology bear a closer resemblance to the first than the second generation of Chicago fieldworkers. These two approaches overlap in their use and advocacy of such techniques as participating in members' activities, exploiting prior membership, penetrating fronts, using covert roles, and cross-checking subjects' accounts against other accounts, direct experience, or documents.

ETHNOMETHODOLOGY: BECOMING THE PHENOMENON

Ethnomethodology derives its intellectual roots from the Parsonian theory of action and the phenomenological philosophy of Edmund Husserl and Alfred Schutz. Phenomenological analysis is oriented toward explicating the world of human thought and conscious experience. Both Schutz and Husserl seek to understand how human consciousness becomes organized into the everyday actor's "natural standpoint" (Husserl, 1962), or commonsense attitude, and how this, in turn, reflects back on the nature of consciousness. Husserl (1962, 1965, 1970) attempts to create a science for studying consciousness by separating out people's everyday situational experiences and reflections, and focusing on the essence of their natural standpoint, or base of pure consciousness. He thus engages in a reductionism designed to discover the essential structures and features of the "transcendental ego," that part of human consciousness that all people share in common, and that underlies all their experiences and social worlds. Schutz (1962, 1964, 1966, 1967), in contrast, attempts to understand how human consciousness is applied in everyday life situations, by forging a systematic description of the natural attitude. This, he believed, would serve as the foundation for understanding the commonsense everyday world of the individual. Schutz advocates that a close description of conscious experience is necessary to understand how people make sense out of and create meaning in their everyday lives. Thus, in contrast to sociology, an empirical discipline the subject matter of which consists primarily of the observable regularities in people's behavior, Husserl's and Schutz's phenomenology is a method for investigating the inner "contours of consciousness" (Freeman, 1980: 114-130).

Ethnomethodology draws heavily on the concerns of phenomenology, fusing Schutz's and Husserl's conceptions of intersubjectivity and the natural attitude with Parsons's question of how social relations come to be patterned and persistent. Harold Garfinkel, the central figure in the ethnomethodological perspective, pioneered this approach during the 1950s and 1960s. He focused ethnomethodology on the cognitive "problem of order," or how people, in their everyday lives, make sense out of, ascribe meaning to, and create a social structure of the world through a process of continual negotiation and interpretation (Cuff and Payne, 1984; Garfinkel, 1967; Heritage, 1984).

Ethnomethodology often appears confusing and mysterious to students of this perspective. This is caused, in part, by the fragmentation of its practitioners. One way of bifurcating the field is to differentiate the "conversational analysts" from the "situational analysts" (Cuff and Payne, 1984: 184). The former pursue formal descriptions of interactional structures, often under the rubric of cognitive sociology (Cicourel, 1964, 1974a, 1974b; Schegloff and Sacks, 1974). The latter study the nature of practical reasoning in everyday situations (Bittner, 1967; Garfinkel, 1952, 1967; Pollner, 1970; Sudnow, 1972, 1978; Weider, 1974; Zimmerman, 1970). While a variety of methods have been employed by ethnomethodologists, the use of participation observation fieldwork (as one of several methods) is generally associated with the latter group.[4] Our discussion, then, will focus on their theoretical stance toward it.

Garfinkel once defined ethnomethodology as beginning with a set of obstinate, unavoidable troubles to the interpretive process—what in Yiddish is called *tsoris*—that do not go away (Leiter, 1980: 107). The primary *tsoris* are indexicality and reflexivity. Each has profound ramifications for ethnomethodological epistemology.

Indexicality and the problematics of outsiders' interpretations. Ethnomethodologists use the concept of indexicality to refer to the highly "occasioned," or contextual nature of objects and events. Without a precise situational context, the interpretations of talk, behavior, and objects are open to multiple or ambiguous meanings. In order to understand the meaning of social action, the following features of the surrounding context must be known to the researcher: (1) the identity of actors, (2) salient aspects of actors' biographies, (3) the actors' immediate intentions and aims, (4) the settings where action occurs, (5) the relationship between actors and their audiences, and (6) how their action "follows" previous action by other participants (Bar-Hillel, 1954; Cicourel, 1974b; Garfinkel, 1967; Husserl, 1969; Leiter, 1980). Everyday life actors' use of the "documentary method of interpretation" (Garfinkel, 1967; Mannheim, 1952) heightens the indexical character of behavior and expressions: People make sense out of the "gloss," of description of an event that others produce, based on their knowledge of each others' past experiences. Researchers must therefore have a close sense of the members' history, how it affects their present, and how they anticipate that the future will influence their retrospective interpretations of objects and events (Garfinkel, 1980).

Indexicality suggests that researchers cannot gain a valid sense of the contextual meanings attached to talk, behavior, and objects unless they participate in their settings to the fullest degree. Researchers, then, who are not complete members can never be fully cognizant of the members' world. As outsiders, they can attain no more than a mere approximation of members' meanings and their understandings of everyday life events. This definition of outsiders includes both traditional Chicago School fieldworkers as well as existential sociologists.

Reflexivity and field research. The reflexivity of people's everyday functioning serves as the second factor, making it difficult for social scientists to apply traditional logic in studying everyday reasoning (how people make sense out of their world) (Handel, 1982). Ethnomethodologists assert that all accounts are reflexive: they are both influenced by the indexical character of the situations that produce them and, in turn, reflect back onto those situations once they are produced. In reflecting back, they subtly (or dramatically) construct those situations by their interpretations of them. As a result of this reciprocal, reflexive relationship, social facts (the orderliness of activities), and the conditions that generate them, are seen as the products of interpretation.

As a result, ethnomethodologists argue that traditional fieldwork methods reflexively influence the worlds they study. In fact, they do more than just influence these worlds—they constitute them. Various methods in the social sciences thus constitute the world in different ways, as Garfinkel et al. (1981: 133) note in recounting Shils and Strodtbeck's disagreement over the procedure to be used in analyzing jury deliberations.[5] Traditional Chicago School fieldwork with its detached participant observation, for instance, constitutes the world in a way that is "experience far" as opposed to "experience near" (Geertz, 1973) by depicting the outsider's perspective. While some of the more recent modifications of symbolic interactionism, such as existential sociology, come closer to attaining the member's perspective, they never come close enough to be acceptable to ethnomethodologists (Garfinkel, 1980).

The only way researchers can avoid constituting the social world differently from the way members do, and thereby attain "thick description" (Geertz, 1973), is to abandon their social scientific allegiances. They must cast off the methodological and theoretical concerns of social science. Researchers who enter their settings with sociological concepts and theoretical frameworks can never understand members' meanings at the level of the members. Ethnomethodologists, thus, ultimately reject traditional field methods and their inherent social science concepts as irremediably problematic. These notions are only excess baggage that obfuscate the fieldworkers' intended mission.

Fieldworker as member: the search for first-order interpretations. Traditional field researchers differ from members because the former engage in theoretical reflections and analyses (Schutz, 1967). According to ethnomethodologists, this distances researchers from both the phenomena and the members' natural standpoint. Bittner (1973: 121) suggests that this distance comes from traditional field researchers' lack of commitment to their settings:

> The paramount fact about the reality bounded by an ethnographic work project is that it is not the field worker's own, actual life situation. This is not because he might disdain accepting it as his own world, nor because he somehow fails in his attempt to make it his world, but because he *cedes* it as not being his world. He has deliberately undertaken to view it as the world of others. . . . In other words, for the fieldworker things are never naturally themselves but only *specimens* of themselves.

Traditional field researchers, then, are inhibited by the fact that they are trained and taught to study others, rather than themselves. They can enter into the members' world, become participants, even become insiders of sorts, but they are always aware that it is not fully their world. For instance, in our study of college athletes, although Peter worked as an assistant coach, he knew that this world was not actually his. Unlike the other assistant coaches, his financial well-being and livelihood was not rooted in the athletic department; instead, he was still being paid for his professorial position. Since he was not dependent upon the basketball team for his job, this allowed him to distance himself from them when necessary. He always knew that when the pressures mounted, he could quit the study, or at least temporarily remove himself from the setting, until the crisis had passed. Ethnomethodologists, then, would reject this membership role as not being truly complete. To always have this "out" meant that he could only approximate, but not totally immerse himself in, the members' world.

In contrast to the controlled feelings and judgments of researchers, members act naturally in their social world. That is not to say, however, that they do not theorize about their world. They continually form and revise commonsense theories, or constructs, of the reality of daily life; it is these practically oriented constructs that determine their behavior (Schutz, 1962). According to Schutz (1962: 6), these theories are "first-order constructs," from which the theories and methodologies of social scientists are, at least, one step removed:

> The constructs used by the social scientists are, so to speak, constructs of the second degree, namely constructs of the constructs made by the actors on the social scene, whose behavior the scientist observes and tries to explain in accordance with the procedural rules of his science.

To overcome the problems of reflexivity (i.e., the distortion of members' worlds by outside frames of reference, theoretical perspectives, and the methods of the social sciences) and indexicality (i.e., outsiders' inability to understand the subjectivity of members' experiences unless they enter into them), ethnomethodologists insist that researchers become members of their settings. Only by becoming actual practitioners in members' social worlds and abandoning the concern for social scientific concepts can researchers understand members' perspectives. Rather than constituting a problem, then, going native is the solution. Researchers should not cede these worlds as somebody else's (Bittner, 1973), but should take them on themselves. This involves making a "good faith" commitment (Garfinkel, 1980) to the life-world, or *lebenswelt* (Schutz, 1964), of everyday life actors and "becoming the phenomenon" (Mehan and Wood, 1975) they wish to study. Researchers who participate in settings, even if they adopt some sort of insider role for sociological purposes, simply do not enter enough into "the experience." As we saw earlier, this is only a limited, "part-time" approximation of the members' lives. Consequently, these researchers do not know the world as members know it. Here, ethnomethodologists make a firm distinction between the methods of existential sociology and their own. Role-playing and using deceptive strategies in the interests of sociological inquiry (see Douglas, 1976; Johnson, 1975; Lofland, 1976;

Peshkin, 1984) do not constitute a good faith commitment. Researchers must make a total commitment to being members and investing their past, present, and future in the setting, thereby lessening their involvement with the social scientific perspective. For instance, in Altheide's (1976: 197) existential sociological study of television news stations, he describes his research experiences as follows:

> My studies of news were done through participant-observation in several settings. My aim was to understand how newsworkers saw their jobs, and how they actually did their work. This entailed spending a considerable amount of time with them covering and reporting news stories. . . . My visits were restricted to several times a week in the early months of observation, since I was preparing for my Ph.D. comprehensive examinations and had to teach part-time to support my wife and daughter.

From an ethnomethodological perspective, Altheide was not making a total, good faith commitment. His primary concerns were still his family and his commitment to social science. An ethnomethodologist would urge this person to secure a job on a television news staff and become a member in the fullest sense of the word. Only then can fieldworkers' commitments become aligned with the domain of the phenomena (beliefs, life-style, and so on), rather than to the theoretical concerns of professional sociologists (Garfinkel, 1980; Mehan and Wood, 1975).

The search for first-order interpretations has caused ethnomethodologists to reject the falsely known social worlds portrayed by traditional ethnographic studies of everyday life. They have taken as their task the rediscovery of these social worlds from the members' perspectives. As Garfinkel et al. (1981: 132-133) note in one of their pioneering essays from the studies-of-work program:

> There exists a distinction in available studies of the discovering work of scientists between studies that make "mentions" of their work ("studies *about* their work") and studies that deliver "material exhibits of work in sequentially developed and technical details" ("studies *of* their work"). . . . Studies *about* discovering scientists' work are commonplace; studies *of* their work are rare [emphasis in original].

Ethnomethodologists thus offer studies of members' work instead of studies about members' work. Let us illustrate this distinction with two examples.

Becker's (1963) study of jazz musicians is a classic example of a traditional symbolic interactionist analysis. From it we learn many features of the life-style of jazz musicians—how they are recruited, what they do, the structure of their social relations and social world, and so on—except how they play music. In contrast, Sudnow (1978: xiii) offers an ethnomethodological analysis: "a close description of the handicraft of improvisation, of the knowing ways of the jazz body . . . on the way toward the closer study of the human body and its works." His work details "the viewpoint of the actor, not through an introspective consciousness, but by a fine examination of concrete problems posed by the task of sustaining an orderly activity" (1978: xiii). Sudnow's work, then, illuminates the practical experience of members' work as the members know and do it.

Qualitative studies of religious conversion provide another example of this distinction. Examples of the classic ethnographic perspective are the studies of Lofland (1966) and Lofland and Stark (1965). These works offer a description of how Divine Precepts live, work, recruit members, and strive to make ready for the New Age. They posit a seven-point analytical model of how individuals become committed to religious groups. From these works we learn how people become members of religious organizations, but we never actually learn about the experience of conversion. In contrast, Jules-Rosette (1975, 1976) presents us with a detailed account of how she underwent religious conversion and became personally transformed. Her focus is on the conversion experience: its reshaping of her inner vision, her new experience of herself, her difficulties in coping after she returned to the West, and the ongoing nature of her transformation. We see again how ethnomethodologists enter into the members' experience and describe it in phenomenological detail.

Just as ethnomethodologists reject the theories and methods of traditional fieldwork, so too are some of them "indifferent" toward the community of sociologists as an audience for their work (Garfinkel and Sacks, 1970). These ethnomethodologists reject the idea of publishing their work in social science sources exclusively; the sociological community is neither the sole target nor the only judge of their research findings (Garfinkel, 1980). Rather, ethnomethodologists argue in favor of orienting their presentations to members. As Mehan and Wood (1975: 228) note:

> The validity of an inquiry is not tested against the corpus of scientific knowledge. It is tested against the everyday experience of a community of people. . . . When members' "moral facts" become their moral facts, researchers will know they have become members.

The appropriate channel for ethnomethodological reports is to "take them back to the field," either by presenting them personally to the individuals studied, or by publishing them in members' journals. This will help to overcome the vast "irrelevance of the topics, methods, findings, and problems" of most social science research for practitioners (Garfinkel et al., 1981).[6] Thus in Rochford's (1983) study of the "crutches" used by stutterers during social interaction, he published his findings in the *Journal of Communication Disorders,* a publication whose readership is primarily speech therapists. The true test of this, and all ethnomethodological studies, then, is the members' assessment of whether it has captured the "quiddity" or "just this-ness" (Garfinkel et al., 1981) of their experience.

The ethnomethodological epistemology stands as the most radical rejection of traditional field research, advocating the most committed and involved stance on the part of fieldworkers.

Synthesis

Since its inception as a sociological method in the 1940s and 1950s, the epistemology of participant observation has evolved considerably. The recent advances of ethnomethodology and existential sociology provide a new perspective for the epistemology of qualitative research. Their views of the data-gathering process suggest that the research act is more problematic than the Chicago School had envisioned.

THE CRITIQUE OF TRADITIONAL FIELD RESEARCH

Both ethnomethodologists and existential sociologists believe that Chicago School participant observers are too "absolutist" in their approach to field research. By emphasizing detachment and objectivity, traditional field researchers espouse the principle of *subject-object dualism*: the belief that the subject (knower) and the object (known) can be effectively separated by methodologically scientific procedures (Douglas, 1976; Hunt, 1984). Ethnomethodologists and existential sociologists reject this claim. They believe that the ideal of objectifying observation is a lingering throwback to the absolutist empiricism of positivist sociological and anthropological thought, which dominated epistemological thinking during the 1940s and 1950s. Chicago School fieldworkers either subtly bought the arguments of objectivist science or tried to bootleg them onto an ostensibly subjectivist methodology in order to gain acceptance, recognition, and/or prestige in the social science community.

Ethnomethodologists and existential sociologists believe, instead, that scientific procedure is a "relativist" endeavor (Douglas, 1970, 1976; Douglas and Johnson, 1977; Feyerabend, 1972; Johnson, 1975; Kauffman, 1944; Mehan and Wood, 1975; Phillips, 1974). They deny the premise of subject-object dualism, claiming that an absolute separation of the knowing subject and the objects of knowledge is impossible. All human knowledge is fundamentally influenced by the subjective character of the human beings who collect and interpret it. In fact, despite claims to the contrary, even the most "objective" methods (i.e., survey research) are influenced by people's interpretive abilities (Cicourel, 1964; Douglas, 1976). Certainly, participant observation, the least controlled mode of gathering data, must be recognized as ultimately grounded in human subjectivity (see Peshkin, 1985).

In addition, existential sociologists and ethnomethodologists reject the idea that researchers should not influence their settings. Much like the notion of remaining objective, influencing settings is a relative, rather than absolute, concept in field research; it is an inevitable outgrowth of researchers interacting with setting members (see Burgess, 1982; Schwartz and Jacobs, 1979). Ultimately, researchers can only weigh the extent and kinds of influences they will permit themselves to exert. Peshkin (1984), for example, decided that he could accept the implicit influence he might have on the fundamentalist Christian students he studied by the fact of his being a visible, even likable, non-born-again Christian. As such, he represented an alternative to the absolutism of their dogmatic teachings. He decided he could not, however, enter into a counseling relationship with a student who had doubts about his or her faith, because that would exceed the bounds of behavior the school authorities could condone and that he had committed himself to observe. Using Freilich's (1970) distinction between the "human" and "research" dimensions of the participant observer, Peshkin concludes that such decisions involve researchers making conscious, albeit partial, limitations to their human selves in the participant observer role. Ethnomethodologists base their decisions about the kinds of influences they feel comfortable allowing on the researchers' degree of commitment to settings. Good faith members will only alter settings in ways similar to other members, so their actions are condoned. Researchers who fall short of this commitment reconstitute their settings according to outside frames of reference, and thus impose an unacceptable influence.

Reciprocally, ethnomethodologists and existential sociologists also believe that researchers' selves are liable to be influenced by the settings they study. Unlike quantitative sociologists, who use questionnaires and/or experiments to gather data, qualitative sociologists rely on their selves as a major research instrument. They must use their human and interactional qualities to gain people's trust and/or attain membership. This often involves opening themselves up to members, while undergoing profound or meaningful experiences with them. Field researchers may, therefore, be fundamentally affected and changed by the research process (Emerson, 1983; Mehan and Wood, 1975; Reinharz, 1979; Wax, (1971).

MEMBERSHIP ROLES IN FIELD RESEARCH

In constructing a taxonomy of researchers' involvement with their settings and subjects, we see that ethnomethodology and existential sociology fall at different points along the spectrum (see Figure 1). We first see the range of roles generally advocated by the classic fieldwork perspective: direct observation of members' talk and behavior; direct, albeit detached, interaction with members; and firsthand participation in some of the members' activities. Existential sociologists advocate more deeply involved roles, urging researchers to shed detachment, draw on their own subjective experiences, and investigate behind the fronts individuals and groups present. At the extreme end, ethnomethodologists require researchers to make a total commitment to becoming the phenomenon in order to study it.

While the ethnomethodological research role comes closer to the phenomenon, it carries with it several problems. Most critically, it is very difficult, if not impossible, to attain. Researchers are asked to "do a reality as its members do" (Mehan and Wood, 1975: 227), yet even the most

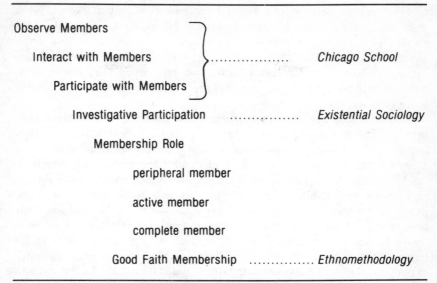

Figure 1   The Continuum of Field Research Involvement

dedicated ethnomethodologist may find it difficult to refrain from theoretical reflection (Jules-Rosette, 1976). In addition, they are asked to conduct research in a way that often requires "disengagement from family, job, and friends" (Mehan and Wood, 1975: 229), a sacrifice most researchers are unwilling to make. Casting off the conceptual concerns of sociology is also difficult, especially for individuals who have struggled to earn their doctorates. For those who hold academic positions, this mandate may be professionally impractical or untenable, as it could result in their losing their jobs. Thus the extreme position of the ethnomethodologists is undesirable for many people committed to job, family, the discipline, and practical matters of everyday life. What remains attractive is the ethnomethodological commitment to search for the "near" experience of members' prescriptions and to generate "thick" description.

We believe that a synthesis of the epistemological positions of ethnomethodology and existential sociology can combine the most desirable features of each. Here we propose an additional category of involvement between researchers and their subjects: *the membership role*. While it is not an altogether new tack, methodologically, it has never been solely advocated epistemologically.

To study social life, it is incumbent upon researchers, whenever possible, to adopt some sort of membership role in the scenes they study. We are not necessarily arguing that researchers can only assume full-time, complete involvement in the scene. Just as some members engage in more central, critical forms of the group's activities than others, so, too, can sociologists take varying kinds of membership roles. They may become involved in either *peripheral, active,* or *complete* membership roles.[7] They may adopt an existing membership role, or carve out a new one, much like we did in our study of college athletes. As Junker (1960) first proposed, these membership roles may evolve and change over time, depending upon changes in the members, the setting, or the researcher. Researchers are also more free to select a certain membership role when they are pointed downward in society's hierarchy rather than upward, where boundaries are more guarded and passages blocked.

The advantage of taking a membership role over other forms of research involvement lies in members' recognition of the researcher as a fellow member. This allows the researcher to participate in the routine practices of members, as one of them, to naturalistically experience the members' world. Doing "membership work" forces the researcher to take on the obligations and liabilities of members. In repeatedly dealing with the practical problems members face, researchers ultimately organize their behavior and form constructs about the setting's everyday reality in much the same way as members. Thus, in contrast to ethnomethodologists, we believe that individuals who fall short of total commitment can still experience the perspective of the members' natural attitude. In fact, human beings are asked to hold and experience the realities of several memberships simultaneously all the time as part of their routine everyday lives. Just as people add their present selves to their collection of previously experienced selves as they age, researchers can add their membership role to their continually expanding role repertoire. A final advantage of taking on a membership role is that researchers can gain access to "secret" information (Junker, 1960: 35). This information, known only to members, ratifies the solidarity and continued existence of the group. Its possession, thus, further reinforces researchers' membership roles.

The epistemological mandate to seek membership roles goes beyond the methodology of existential sociology in three ways. First, it requires that researchers take or carve a membership role in their settings, whether this constitutes a peripheral, active, or complete membership role. Second, the researchers' own perspectives, experiences, and emotions become equally important to the accounts gathered from others, instead of serving as an important, but secondary, enhancement. This highlights the importance of researchers' subjectivity, casting it as an unabashed virtue (see Peshkin, 1985). Finally, we advocate opening membership audiences as acceptable outlets for researchers' work. Although the sociological community remains the primary outlet, ethnographic insights should be used to educate or aid the practitioners in whose settings the research was conducted.

The epistemological advocacy of membership roles thus represents a critical synthesis of the evolving everyday life sociologies. As such, it may also formally codify a range of roles and procedures that have been practiced informally by many Chicago School researchers for years. While these fieldworkers have implicitly recognized the need for getting close to their phenomena and for adapting their role to the structure and demands of the settings they studied (Gans, 1985), it is now time for fieldwork epistemology to be modified to reflect this practical, taken-for-granted orientation. We therefore formally advocate that researchers adopt membership roles in the settings they study.

In the remainder of the book we will examine the characteristics of each membership role in detail. The focus of Chapter Two is the peripheral membership role, the least involved of the three roles. Peripheral-member-researchers participate as insiders in the activities of the group they are studying, but they refrain from engaging in the most central activities. In Chapter Three we consider the active membership role, where researchers participate in the core activities in much the same way as members, yet they hold back from committing themselves to the goals and values of members. The complete membership role is the subject of Chapter Four. Complete-member-researchers study their topics from the perspective of full members by either selecting groups to study in which they have prior membership or by converting to membership in these groups. Within these chapters, we describe and illustrate the stages and features of each role, drawing on a limited number of examples to clarify and highlight the experiences we outline. We begin each chapter by considering the process of becoming a member and some of the factors that aid or hinder its occurrence. We then examine various characteristics of the membership experience: the nature of each role's research exchange; the various types of role demands they are likely to encounter; the types of relationships that arise between researchers and the members they study; the membership affiliations in which researchers may become enmeshed; changes and shifts in involvement and commitment likely to be encountered by researchers in the different roles; and the character of the disengagement processes. At the conclusion of each chapter we reflect on the effects these membership roles have on both the data-gathering process and the researcher's self. We close the book with a brief epilogue where we consider implications of the membership methodology.

NOTES

1. Faught (1980) has argued, however, that the major presuppositions of the Chicago School were given continuity in the work and teachings of Everett Hughes.

2. Platt (1983) has documented the uses of the term *participant observation* that occurred prior to this era. She notes, however, that these usages in the 1930s represented a process wherein participant observation was disengaging itself from earlier ideas and was not yet seen as a distinct method in its own right.

3. The relationship between participant observation fieldwork and the theoretical perspective of symbolic interactionism is a topic of disagreement and debate among sociologists. Rock (1979) and Shalin (1986) argue that participant observation is an outgrowth of symbolic interactionism, yet many of Hughes's students maintain that the two are essentially unconnected (Gans, 1985). Regardless of their formal linkage, we would argue that the two draw upon fundamentally compatible views of the individual and society. We will use the term *symbolic interactionism* hereafter to refer to the theoretical framework backing participant observation epistemology, not because we are taking a position in this debate but because it is simpler and because it and Hughes's situational and structural perspective are not significant to our discussion.

4. It is also significant to note that the use of participant observation and situational analysis has declined among ethnomethodologists in the 1980s. Most practitioners have turned to the more objective and detached methods associated with sociolinguistics (videotaping, audio taping, conversation analysis) in their search for the micro social structure embedded in natural language.

5. Edward Shils was part of a committee at the University of Chicago Law School that hired Fred Strodtbeck, in 1954, to analyze tape recordings of jury deliberations. Strodtbeck proposed administering the Bales Interaction Process Analysis, to which Shils countered, "By using Bales Interaction Process Analysis I'm sure we'll learn what about a jury's deliberations makes them a small group. But we want to know what about their deliberations makes them a jury" (Garfinkel et al., 1981: 133).

6. Two sources of irony and contradiction present themselves here, which we can only remark upon but not resolve. First, due to the evolving fragmentation within the perspective, these beliefs do not represent the attitudes of all ethnomethodologists (see Maynard, 1986). Second, there is a disparity between what these ethnomethodologists preach and what they practice. While Garfinkel argues against presenting his findings to the social science community, he has done just that (see Garfinkel et al., 1981). And while Mehan and Wood (1975) advocate becoming the phenomenon, the primary methodology used by the former is videotaping.

7. These categories are necessarily ideal typical. There are, of course, times when they overlap, shift in character, or become dislodged from their positions on the continuum. This is often the result of situational or personal occurrences in the setting, over which researchers have little control. They are intended, however, to illustrate heuristically a range of behaviors that commonly combine to form a research stance.

2. PERIPHERAL MEMBERSHIP

Of the three membership role categories, the peripheral role is the most marginal and least committed to the social world studied. Researchers who assume this role, though, feel that some sort of membership is desirable to gain an accurate appraisal of human group life. They seek an insider's perspective on the people, activities, and structure of the social world, and feel that the best way to acquire this is through direct, first-hand experience. They interact closely, significantly, and frequently enough to acquire recognition by members as insiders. They do not, however, interact in the role of central members, refraining from participating in activities that stand at the core of group membership and identification. As a result, they generally do not assume functional roles within the group.

Peripheral-member-researchers (PMRs) may hold back or be restricted from more central membership roles for several reasons. First, they may intentionally limit their involvement with the group because of epistemological beliefs. They may be able to become a part of the scene, or one group within it, but hold themselves back from being overly drawn in because they fear it will damage their ability to interpret the data they observe detachedly. Second, researchers may intentionally restrict their level of membership because they do not wish to participate in the specific activities of the group they are studying. This is particularly prevalent among researchers who are gathering data on deviant groups, such as our research on upper-level drug dealers and smugglers. Here our decision to refrain from trafficking, due to the obvious danger, restricted us to a marginal membership status. We became close friends with several central participants, we socialized regularly with them and their social set (girlfriends, wives, employees), and we became accepted members of their social scene—in other words, we could be vouched for as trustworthy, but could never be considered full members. Third, researchers may be blocked from more central membership by their demographic characteristics (age, race, sex, religion, social class, and so on) and/or their assumed norms and values. Peshkin (1984), for example, remained a peripheral member throughout his study of Bethany, a fundamentalist Christian church and school, despite the fact that for nearly two years he lived at a church member's home and participated on a daily basis in the school's academic, athletic, and social functions. His marginality was not due to his overt research role or the community's distrust of him, but rather that, as a Jew, he could not accept his subjects' faith. Similarly, in LeMasters's (1975) research on a blue-collar tavern, he was a regular patron of the establishment for five years and served as a member of the tavern's pool team for the last three of those years. He was blocked from anything more than peripheral membership, however, by his academic occupation and middleclass background. Simply, he was too different from his subjects to be` anything but peripheral. Any combination of these three factors can lead researchers to assume a peripheral membership role. In Horowitz's (1983) study of a Chicano youth gang, for example, her age (older), dress code (less stylish), and nonparticipation in the group's dangerous or sexual activities caused the gang members to define her as a "lady." Yet, because she hung out in the park with them daily, on weekends, and after dark, asking them questions for the book she claimed to be writing, they gradually redefined her role to "lady reporter," the group's personal chronicler. Like other peripheral members, she became "with" but not "part of" or "like" the group.

Generally, PMRs' relationships with setting members involve daily or near-daily contact. They may live with members, as Peshkin did, or they may take members into their homes to live with them temporarily, as we did when one of our key informants showed up on our doorstep, penniless, after being released from prison. This is not usually the case, however. In most instances, PMRs do not live with members; they try, instead, to maintain some distance between themselves and the people they study, as in the cases of LeMasters and Horowitz. They freely entered and left the setting whenever they wanted. The episodic character of the participation and presence led members to develop only limited expectations of them. This distance is especially critical to researchers who do not want to be drawn into closer membership roles, yet whose potential similarity to their subjects leaves them vulnerable to such recruitment. PMRs, thus, usually occupy one of two types of roles within their settings. They may take the role of a "social" member, or they may forge their own "researcher-member" role. LeMasters and we adopted the former, becoming accepted as regulars in the social crowd without participating in the central functions of the group (which were occupational, in both of these cases). The latter strategy was pursued by Peshkin and Horowitz, who espoused avowedly overt roles and came to be labeled as researchers accepted by and affiliated with the group. They thus created roles for themselves, based on a combination of their interests and members' conceptions of possible identity categories.

PMRs develop relationships with members that vary in kind and intensity. These can run the gamut from acquaintanceship with some members to close friendship with key informants. PMRs can develop the trust and acceptance of their respondents in several ways. Some use the approval of a gatekeeper, as Marquart (1983) did in his initial phase of studying prison guards within a maximum security penitentiary. Working as a researcher on a project evaluating staff supervision, training, and turnover, he held several meetings with one of the prison wardens. Through this warden, Marquart obtained permission to visit the prison as an employee of the administration-sponsored study and was given unrestricted research access. Alternately, researchers may rely on the sponsorship of one or more members of the setting, as we did in our dealing and smuggling research. Having first befriended our next-door neighbor, we were able to rely on his help in broadening our pool of subjects. He introduced us to his friends and vouched for us as trustworthy and reliable. A third approach involves researchers drawing on their personal familiarity and/or friendship with their subjects, as Hoffman (1980) was forced to do in her study of the elite governing boards of hospitals in the province of Quebec. She first tried to gain entrée through traditional, impersonal means (i.e., letters of introduction, phone calls, appointments for interviews), but found that she got nothing more than a brush-off and an occasional bit of carefully screened frontwork. After considerable fruitless time spent in the field, she inadvertently realized the value of her (previously unmentioned) peripheral membership with her subjects (she was from their elite social class) when one of her respondents discovered during an interview that he was friendly with members of her family. Immediately, the character of the interview changed and she obtained data that were dramatically different from all that she had gathered during previous efforts. From then on, she exploited her peripheral membership to obtain interviews and establish rapport. Reflecting on the value of both her friendship ties and peripheral membership in enhancing her data gathering, Hoffman (1980: 48-50) states:

> Friendship norms were factors in my new-found access. In general, the closer the friendship tie with members of my family, the less frequently informants postponed or canceled interviews with me and the more inside information they allowed me. . . . Friendship ties reduced the perceived risk associated with confiding in me by acting as a form of security that information would

not be misused or that boards would not be portrayed in an unfavorable light. . . .

Although I myself was not a board member, or a businessman, or even of the same generation as my respondents, I reaped some of the benefits of inside status by virtue of belonging to their social class—an attribute the data indicated was central to their role and function as board members. As with friendship, common class membership increased the level of trust in our relationship over any that I could create as an unknown interviewer.

Despite these ties, PMRs are likely to be acutely aware of differences between members and themselves. Faced with the intimate details and inner feelings of their subjects, as any participant observation research requires, PMRs may find themselves confronted by members' activities that they can rationally describe and analyze, but never fully grasp emotionally. For instance, in our drug dealing research, our respondents could never fathom how, given our extensive knowledge of drug buyers and sellers in the area, we could resist the temptation to deal. We, in turn, had trouble understanding how they could spend their last several hundred dollars on an evening of partying when they owed the money to the landlord or some other dealer the next day, or how individuals could repeatedly do business with associates they knew to be unreliable, losers, or "rip-off artists." Such differences between researchers and members are likely to be greater for PMRs than for active or complete researchers, because the latter are often personally, demographically, or experientially more compatible with their subjects.

PMRs also vary in the extent of their involvement with and commitment to settings and their members. While they strive to develop empathy, they make a conscious effort to limit their involvement and commitment. Horowitz, for example, found that she had to define herself repeatedly as ineligible for dates with male gang members or for sponsorship roles with the female gang when the latter needed transportation to or assistance with fights. This kind of involvement would have destroyed her identity as a "lady" and barred her from gathering certain types of data. PMRs are commonly detached from the people they study, however, by virtue of both their marginal participation in the group's activities and the differences between themselves and members. They thus have few problems retaining their academic self-identity, and experience limited role conflict between their researcher and membership roles.

The Process of Membership

The research experience of PMRs differs from nonmember researchers as well as from researchers involved in more central membership roles.

BECOMING A PERIPHERAL-MEMBER-RESEARCHER

There are several factors that can influence researchers to adopt a peripheral membership role in conducting fieldwork. First, they may have a natural affinity for the group and/or the activity involved. For instance, based on our prior research in the drug world (see Cummins et al., 1972) and participation in the hippie subculture, we were familiar with and nonjudgmental toward the activities, vernacular, and life-style displayed by our subjects. Second, as we mentioned earlier, some researchers epistemologically favor developing close relationships with their subjects, but also feel that this involvement should be tempered by certain restraints against overinvolvement. The peripheral role, then, offers them the best vantage for conducting research. Third, researchers may begin with a detached stance but be drawn, by members, into more involved roles (Pollner and Emerson, 1983). For example, researchers who exploit their personal qualities to gain subjects' trust and their intimate disclosures may find that subjects expect a reciprocity of shared intimacies and personal involvement. These researchers are often enticed out of guilt, obligation, or friendship into an active participatory role in their subjects' lives, although they may continue to refrain from participating in the groups' core activities. Finally, researchers may assume a peripheral membership role because of the specific character of their empirical setting. Some settings allow the presence of outsiders only in certain roles. Rochford (1985), for example, in his research on Hare Krishnas, found that he could not study the group without committing, at minimum, to a peripheral membership role. In contrast, some settings are either so highly secretive or so exclusive that they bar researchers from attaining anything closer than a peripheral membership role. This was the case in Corsino's (1984) study of a political campaign, in which he was relegated to a menial volunteer role because he lacked the commitment, connections, and political interests/aspirations necessary to gain access to the campaign's inner sanctum.

THE MEMBERSHIP EXPERIENCE

Once the researcher has taken on a peripheral membership role, the research experience involves a patterned flow of occurrences. The first of these is the *research exchange*. Unlike Corsino, who offered his subjects little, and even complained about the volunteer tasks he was asked to do, most researchers are sensitive to the norms of reciprocity and exchange inherent in the fieldwork process. Field researchers are motivated to forge either formal or informal and patterned or occasional exchanges with their field respondents for various reasons. First, an exchange of information and services may be something that is explicitly arranged when the researcher's entrée is being negotiated. Second, even without this formal obligation, researchers may feel it incumbent upon themselves to offer something back to their respondents in exchange for all the intrusion and probing they are doing and the data they are receiving. Third, researchers may manipulatively try to use these norms of reciprocity to their advantage by doing favors for their respondents and only accepting "repayment" in the form of research assistance (Douglas, 1976, 1985).

Qualitative researchers establish different types of research exchanges, depending on their role in the setting. PMRs, by virtue of their nonparticipation in the group's central activities, are excluded from the equal role reciprocity of most active or complete members. Since they do not offer their full commitment to the group, their feelings of being parasites may be exacerbated. This may lead them to offer a variety of noncentral participation: advice, favors, professional services, and friendship. In our study of drug trafficking, for example, we not only housed our key informant for seven months, but over the six years we were involved in the research we also fed him, clothed him, took care of his children, wrote letters of reference on his behalf, helped to organize his criminal defense, visited him in jail, gave him money, and testified in child support court for him. Despite the somewhat tangential nature of the role, then, the character of PMRs' research exchanges may lead them to develop close personal relationships with their respondents.

A second dimension of this type of research experience involves fieldworkers' *membership relationships.* In gathering data, researchers probe into intimate and personal matters with people whom they might not ordinarily encounter and/or select as friends. They thus relate, often deeply, to people who may be quite different from themselves. This can lead to frustration, as when we repeatedly saw overly trusting or thoughtless dealers losing money on drug deals, but could do nothing to influence their decision making, or when Horowitz's female gang members repeatedly urged her to improve her appearance, but to no avail. A by-product of researchers studying people unlike themselves is that they can experience self-revelations from reflecting on themselves through the members' perspectives. We, for example, had always thought of ourselves as fairly liberal, spontaneous, and generally "cool," but after several years of hanging around with drug traffickers who lived the "fast life," we began to realize how much we needed the security of a monthly paycheck, a well-planned career, freedom from worry about arrest, and a faithful, monogamous marriage; in short, we realized how truly "straight" we were.

Third, PMRs may also have unique *role demands* placed upon them. Although these demands may be more minimal than those placed on active or complete researchers, they are often more difficult for PMRs to negotiate because of the undefined nature of their roles. For instance, while we were never asked to engage in the explicit activities of dealing, transporting, or storing drugs, we had more tacit demands placed on us. We had to guard against insiders' secrets being mistakenly leaked to others, we had to show support for members' "extracurricular" (especially extramarital) activities, and we had to assist dealers in presenting their false legitimate fronts. Our marginality made us especially suspicious, so we were constantly having to prove our trustworthiness. Horowitz, too, was often tested by different gang members who purposely fed her "juicy" but erroneous gossip to see if she was a reliable source to whom they could impart confidences.

Usually these role expectations fall within the established bounds that researchers have forged. There are inevitably instances, however, where members test researchers' limits. The research experience is filled, in this way, with decisions researchers must constantly make to define and redefine their membership roles. Thus the female gang members knew that Horowitz had separated herself from potentially violent or dangerous activities, yet they asked her, on separate occasions, to transport them to a fight and to become their "sponsor." Usually PMRs are able to refuse these requests without jeopardizing their research role, but in some cases this is not possible. Key informants who understand the value of their assistance and of researchers' consequent dependence on them are in a position to exploit researchers. They may thus assert a double standard of behavior in their relations with researchers, holding high expectations of interpersonal commitment and reliability for researchers, while engaging in more dishonorable and self-serving actions themselves. One key informant occasionally exploited us in this way, lying to us, failing to repay money he owed us, and going behind our backs to break security rules that we had established. Such occurrences are structurally generic to peripheral membership relations due to the nature of the research exchange. Just as researchers may actively seek to manipulate members into openness, members are in a position to reciprocate this manipulation to gain researchers' favors, with or without either conscious awareness or guilt.

Fourth, the membership experience may be characterized by *role changes and shifts*. Roles and identities, like trust, are not immutable, but evolving. Thus researchers' roles can fluctuate, changing to different membership categories or shifting in character within the same category. Peripheral members may undergo minor transformations in their roles due to several factors: the ongoing stream of actions and occurrences; structural changes in the setting; the introduction of new members to the setting, and / or changes in their selves. These shifts may be associated with changes in their kind and degree of participation with either the group as a whole or with individuals or factions within it. For example, in the dealing research, when we accepted one of our key informants into our house to live for several months, our relationship with him became much more intimate. However, this alienated his ex-wife, another one of our key informants, who was involved with a different but overlapping set of associates in her own right. We were seen by these dealers as affiliated with him, perhaps on a business level, and shunned by her. It took us several years to recoup our relationship with her and regain her trust, confidence, and research assistance.

Researchers' role shifts are thus not always unidirectional. Some may generate greater involvement with subjects, while others lead to greater detachment. Horowitz (1986: 420-422) describes how a shift in her role created greater distance between the gang members and herself:

> Identities are not fixed but are affirmed or changed continually. It was an
> advantage to be appraised as a lady and a reporter, as that identity allowed

me to maintain a degree of distance and legitimacy as a woman among men. However, the longer I remained with the group, the more I became aware that some of the young men were attempting to redefine my identity as a potential girl-friend, making my sexual identity salient. . . . After fifteen months, their sexual teasing of me increased significantly and several stated that I knew too much about them. . . . I began to be perceived as a threat to the group.

Horowitz's growing knowledge of the gang members' selves behind their front of bravado eventually led to the erosion of her lady reporter identity. Ironically, the closer she became to them as people, the more her intimacy and rapport with them was threatened.

Changes and shifts in researchers' roles can also move them into different membership categories. Peripheral membership is often a transitional role, serving as a point of entry for people who will ultimately move toward closer, more involved roles. During the early phase of Rochford's study of Hare Krishnas, for example, he attempted to observe the group, participate in their social but not religious activities, and get to know the community of devotees. After several months of attending regularly, he found he could no longer study the group through this peripheral membership role. Their pressure on him to convert was so great that he realized he had to either escalate to an active membership role or be forced out of the setting.

The move to a more involved role can also be initiated by the researcher's desires, as we experienced in our study of college athletes (Adler, 1984; Adler and Adler, 1985, forthcoming). Peter, the insider and principal investigator, had attained a peripheral membership role during his first year of studying the team: He had become friendly with the players and coaches; he was granted permission to enter the locker room before and after the games; we were given complimentary game tickets seated behind the team; and he was invited to lecture at the coach's summer camps and clinics. Yet he was uneasy. To be on the periphery can be an awkward and uncomfortable position, especially in a setting where a great deal of emphasis is placed on the distinction between insiders and outsiders. He was plagued by a host of personal and epistemological questions: Did he belong? Where? Why didn't they like him more? Was he close enough to the phenomenon? Was he getting the data he needed? Was he really getting an insider's perspective? Feeling marginal, he sensed that he constantly had to work at proving his worth to the coaches so that he would not slip into the morass of outside sycophants. He therefore decided to press for a more active membership role.

DISENGAGEMENT

The final phase of the membership experience involves researchers either diminishing their involvement to a less committed membership role or withdrawing from the field entirely. From the position of peripheral membership, these two alternatives are closely entwined and may be hard to distinguish, because there is no less committed membership role. Researchers who want to diminish their involvement without quitting the field altogether may do so for a number of reasons. First, they may feel that they have gathered enough data to begin their analysis and writing, but not want to cut off their involvement with their respondents entirely, lest they should discover gaps in their knowledge during the writing phase and need to gather more information. Second, they may wish to continue their membership role and data gathering but be forced by external constraints to taper their involvement. These include the termination of research funds, pressure from family members to spend less time in the field, and demands from colleagues and sponsors to start publishing findings (Snow, 1980).

Changing one's research role from peripheral membership to non-membership participant observation is nearly impossible. From the members' standpoint, they have come to view the researcher's identity through his or her more involved role and they are usually unwilling to accept the researcher on a less committed level. This may be because there are not structurally appropriate nonmembership roles in the setting for the researcher to take/make, or because members feel deserted and angered by the researcher's diminished relationship with them and are unwilling to re-create the relationship on a lesser level. PMRs who want to disengage without leaving the field entirely thus usually shift to a nonparticipant role. They may either continue making detached observations of the scene, or they may make observations and punctuate these with additional depth interviews.

PMRs who want to disengage completely from their field settings may do so for any of the same reasons as those who want merely to diminish their involvement. Two other factors may also prompt their disengagement: problems with setting members or a major change in the setting. In the course of evolving through a development and flux in their relations with setting members, researchers may find that this relationship has gone awry. If this occurs with only one or two individuals, it will not threaten the research, but if the problem is more pervasive it can force termination of the project. For example, in the course of the drug dealing research, we moved too quickly toward asking one "dealer's old lady" to let us interview her on tape; we thought we had gained her trust, but we discovered we were wrong when she evaded all our questions during the interview and feigned excessive sleepiness. She never spoke to us again, but that did not endanger our relationship with any of our other respondents. Horowitz, in contrast, developed a problem that involved all of her respondents. Over the course of her involvement with the male gang, the members began to feel threatened by her intimate knowledge of them, and she began to feel threatened by their attempts to involve her in intimacy:

> I knew too much about them as people—their problems, weaknesses, hopes, and fears. They needed one another and they knew that I knew that. I knew

them too well and was aware they were not all that they publicly claimed to be (tough warriors). . . . As soon as they began to see me as a potential sexual partner, . . . my independence and control through intimate knowledge became problematic to them. . . . As the pressures increased to take a locally defined membership role, I was unable to negotiate a gender identity that would allow me to continue as a researcher [Horowitz, 1986: 422-423].

Horowitz was thus forced out of the setting by the members' changed attitudes toward her, although she retained a relationship with several individual gang members. Problems between researchers and their respondents can arise gradually, as they did for Horowitz, or they can explode, as when researchers using a covert role have their cover blown.

Additionally, researchers may have to leave the setting when it changes in character, either structurally or by population. Some scenes are time bound: They exist as temporary phenomena. Upon their conclusion, the research also ceases. In other cases, the departure or loss of status by a researcher's key informant can prompt the termination of a project. This occurs most often in settings where membership is both (upwardly and downwardly) mobile and transitory.

PMRs who disengage from their field settings usually maintain contact with one or more of their key informants, either for the purpose of retaining continued access to the setting or because they have forged strong friendship bonds with these individuals. Horowitz continued to see individual gang members as she started to research community organizations, schools, and politics. This enhanced her return to the field for a follow-up study of the gang seven years later, when they acted as though she had never left (Horowitz, 1983). Seven years after we withdrew from actively researching the drug world, had two children, and moved 1,500 miles away, we still saw our key informant once or twice yearly and spoke to him every couple of months. Intrinsic to the nature of any membership role, then, is a heightened difficulty in withdrawing completely from a setting and its members.

Variations in the difficulty researchers can experience in attempting to disengage from their settings are due to two factors: the intensity of the researcher's membership role and the tenacity of the group toward its members. PMRs, compared to active and complete members, clearly have the easiest task in disengaging themselves; they are less central to the functioning of the group and less self-involved in the group. When they leave the field or shift from a participatory to a remote role, they leave less of a void in both the group and themselves.

Based on his own and others' field experiences, Snow (1980) suggests that researchers have different degrees of difficulty in disengaging from the field, which may not be solely due to their various roles in the setting. Rather, this may be related to the characteristics of their communities to "the attitude and policy of the group being studied toward the withdrawal or defection of its members" (p. 109). In groups where membership turnover is anticipated and routine, members react without alarm to researchers' prospective withdrawals, and disengagement can be relatively easily effected. Other groups, though, are not as casual about the entry or departure of their members, clinging to their constituents less they stray from the fold. Thus, as Snow discovered, researchers who assume membership roles in proselytizing social movements, religious sects, and some secret societies may be increasingly recruited and pressured toward greater involvement once they indicate that they are thinking of leaving. Expansionistic groups such as these, however, are less likely to tolerate researchers in peripheral membership roles. The peripheral membership role is more commonly found, then, among groups where people come and go with frequency, and where the reaction to researchers' departures are less anguished.

Reflections

In evaluating the impact of peripheral membership roles, there are several issues that must be addressed. First, researchers may derive *status and/or stigma* from this role. As members, albeit peripheral ones, researchers' identities are often influenced by their contact with the group. This effect varies between inside and outside observers. With outsiders, researchers may experience the "contagion of stigma" (Kirby and Corzine, 1981) and either suffer or benefit from the esteem in which their subjects are held by the general community. On the positive side, researchers may become objects of curiosity and/or envy, as people perceive them to hold interesting or desirous positions near respected groups. The degree of this status is usually modified by the known limitations of researchers' actual involvement with these groups. When researchers study deviant or stigmatized groups, however, no matter how partial the involvement, they must deal with the disdain, mistrust, or revulsion of outsiders. For instance, after leaving the site of our dealing research and moving to a new town, Patti was often asked by our new neighbors and acquaintances about the subject of her impending doctoral thesis. Her indication of the topic and description of the community of upper-level dealers and smugglers brought mildly disguised concern, discreet expressions of shock and disapproval, and increasingly alarmed inquiries into the methods by which the data were gathered. She learned to revise her explanation about her thesis topic in stages, changing it first to some veiled references about a deviant occupation (while implying through nonverbal gestures that it was too complicated for the layperson to understand). When this evasive reply proved either too intriguing or still too stigmatizing, she then merely stated that it was in the area of alcohol and drug abuse. Until she implicitly conveyed a moralistic tone toward the deviant behavior and implied a clear separation between herself and any possible offenders, she was treated by people as an undesirable, a person to be shunned.

Insiders in the setting are neither impressed nor revulsed by researchers' association with their group's activities. Rather, insiders are affected by the degree to which researchers associate with and are accepted by the group, either formally or informally. Here the sanctioning of researchers' presence and their being assigned an insider role by an influential leader or gatekeeper are critical. The membership role thus grants researchers legitimacy within the group and encourages members to trust them. For insiders, however, the degree of membership is carefully noticed; peripheral membership roles will not generate the same amount of trust and access to unconstrained data as will active or complete membership roles.

Peripheral membership roles can also *affect researchers' selves*. Although peripheral members can distance themselves from their setting both physically and psychologically, these effects can, nonetheless, be fairly intense. As we saw earlier, the most common by-products of interacting in this role are new self-revelations and changed self-images. These can also be supplemented by the development of intense feelings and responses, as Peshkin experienced in his study of Bethany, where he developed a research identity and a set of violent emotional reactions that contrasted greatly with his expectations:

> In my fieldwork there was an unexpected occasion to be defined, labelled, and judged, and therefore to learn unexpected things about myself. . . . At Bethany I wanted to be the non-Christian scholar interested in learning about the fundamentalist educational phenomenon that was sweeping the country. I discovered, so to speak, that being Jewish would be the personal fact bearing most on my research; it became the unavoidably salient aspect of my subjectivity. Bethanyites let me define my research self, but could never rest easy with my unsaved self. I became forcibly aware that the threats to my identity as a Jew were not just a matter of history.

> For in the course of inculcating their students with doctrine and the meaning of the Christian identity, Bethany's educators taught us both that I was part of Satan's rejected, humanist world; I epitomized the darkness and unrighteousness that contrasts with their godly light and righteousness. They taught their children never to be close friends, marry, or to go into business with someone like me. What they were expected to do with someone like me was proselytize. . . .

> The Academy's fundamentalist orthodoxy made me concerned about the resultant insularity of its students; its unrelenting evangelical efforts made me concerned about a future society (like those my persecuted ancestors lived in) that contained no place for me as I am. To repeat, Bethany gored me [Peshkin, 1985: 13-15].

The unexpected nature of his self-revelations corresponds to ours in doing the drug study. From that research experience, we gained insight into our fundamental needs, values, and concerns by realizing how different these were from those of our respondents. We left the study with a sense of the innate conservatism and need for security that underlay our casual attitude toward the youth and drug culture.

A final reflection on the peripheral membership role involves its *influences on data gathering*. Because the peripheral role is the least committed and involved, its practitioners may be the least liable to subjective emotional influences coloring their perceptions. Yet, while PMRs may be the least influenced by subjective biases, they also have the least amount of direct participation in core group activities to draw upon as a base of experience. LeMasters (1975), for example, writes about blue-collar workers without ever investigating the area of blue-collar work. The peripheral membership role is the strongest of the three from the classical Chicago perspective, enhancing researchers' ability to gather data from different groups in the setting and then step back to analyze these in a moderately detached manner. At the same time it is the weakest according to ethnomethodological criteria, lacking the members' good faith commitment, core participation, and hindering researchers from truly grasping the members' experience and perspective.

PMRs may also experience data-gathering problems because of their limited involvement in their settings. Their decision to hold back from participating in the core activities of the group may leave members unsure about their identity and commitment. This may make it difficult for PMRs to form relationships with and gain the trust of their respondents. In our drug dealing research, for example, we inspired limited trust beyond our key informants, those individuals with whom we had gone overt and done taped interviews. The setting, in general, was characterized by a sharp insider/outsider distinction because of the highly illegal nature of the activity. Dealers and smugglers spoke fairly openly about their exploits to those whom they considered members of the community, but this mostly included other dealers and their women. The fact that we refrained from dealing cast an air of suspicion around us; not only did we have something "dirty" on them that they did not have on us, but we were suspected, at times, of being narcs.

Hunt (1984; to be discussed in more detail in Chapter 3) also encountered this problem, and describes how the ambiguity and role confusion about her identity in studying the police led her to be perceived initially as a spy:[1]

> When a field-worker first enters a police setting, he is commonly viewed as a "stranger whose loyalty and trustworthiness are suspect." . . . At best the researcher is perceived as a "social critic" . . . who seeks to discredit the police by publicizing compromising details of their occupational life. At worst, he is seen as a "spy" for some external or internal agency involved in a formal investigation of police misconduct. . . .
>
> In my case, the policemen's suspicion that I was an undercover agent for the Internal Affairs Bureau or the FBI was intensified by the political dynamics of the field situation. . . . The department tried to sabotage my relations with the police. They instituted formal rules to ensure my isolation and fostered the view that I was a spy. The word was spread that I would report illegal activity and rank-and-file officers were warned to avoid me.
>
> Even if the department had affirmed my status as an independent researcher, I still would have been suspect, in part because the role of spy was consistent

with my gender identity. As a civilian and a moral woman I represented the formal order of law and the inside world of the academy.... Given my gender and formal orientation, many policemen assumed that I would naively report their activities to the department out of a sense of moral responsibility [Hunt, 1984: 288-289].

Thus, although Hunt attended the academy and went on patrols, she was known to be a consultant hired by the city to evaluate the police, and was considered "with" but not "like" the rank-and-file police. She was unable to overcome this spy stigma and gain the men's confidence until she proved herself both reliable and an ally through her competent handling of police emergencies in the field and by repeatedly taking an antiestablishment stance in the political struggles of the department.

The closest correspondent to this membership role is the participant-as-observer, defined by Gold (1958) as an overt role characterized by more time spent participating than observing. Gold warns about the problems that may arise between "role" and "self" in this stance, positing that overintimacy may negatively influence both the researcher and the researched, leading to a breakdown in their formal roles. The observational role is therefore seen as the data-gathering one, and the participatory role but a means to achieve a better observational vantage point.

The peripheral membership role comprises a similar bifurcation of involvement and detachment, where researchers hold some part of themselves back from joining in with the setting and its members. Because their goals are different from those of the members, and because they may be seen differently by members than they see themselves, PMRs, like participants-as-observers, engage in a good deal of role pretense. When things become too confusing or pressured, they can leave the setting to regenerate.

In many ways, however, the correspondence between these two roles is superficial. PMRs are not mandated to hold their human selves in as sterile a manner, but are urged to use themselves as an additional source of data. The research and personal dimensions are merged more fully, with the data-gathering dimensions affecting the researcher as a person and the human feelings and beliefs spilling over (to an extent) into the setting. The peripheral membership role is also more complex and flexible than that of the participant-as-observer. The covert, as well as overt, stance can be pursued, and social membership, as well as the researcher-member stance, are sought. The involvement with research subjects, thus, can vary enormously.

Peripheral membership, the most detached membership role, thus corresponds to, and goes beyond, the involvement and participation of the participant-as-observer.

NOTE

1. Although Hunt used an active membership role, the problem of trusting the researcher's commitment and identity is far more endemic to the peripheral membership role.

3. ACTIVE MEMBERSHIP

With active membership, the researcher moves clearly away from the marginally involved role of the traditional participant observer and assumes a more central position in the setting. Researchers who adopt active membership roles do more than participate in the social activities of group members; they take part in the core activities of the group (to the extent that these core activities can be defined and agreed upon by group members). In so doing, they generally assume functional, not solely research or social, roles in their settings. Active-member-researchers (AMRs), therefore, relate to members of the setting in a qualitatively different way than do researchers in peripheral membership roles. Instead of merely sharing the status of insiders, they interact as colleagues: coparticipants in a joint endeavor. For example, in our research on college athletics, as mentioned earlier, we used a multiperspectival approach where Peter, the insider and principal investigator, took an active membership role. Patti remained more of a detached outsider, part of the team's social world but not subject to the daily inside experiences and pressures of running the team. He became an assistant coach with the nebulously defined responsibilities of serving as the team's interpersonal counselor, career counselor, and academic advisor. As a member of the coaching staff, he sat on the bench during games, attended practices, booster functions, banquets, and road games, and was called upon to oversee players' schedules, to deal with specific academic problems, and to guide the coaches through the academic maze of the university. He therefore served as an integral cog of the athletic program, assisting in both the routine functioning and crisis mobilizations of the team's activities.

Another active membership role was undertaken by Jennifer Hunt (see Hunt, 1984), who conducted a study of a large, urban police department. During the course of her research, Hunt attended the police academy with male and female recruits and later rode with individual officers in one-man cars during their eight-hour patrol shifts. She also practiced on the pistol range, participated in the arrest and disarming of violent offenders, attended police social functions, and assisted rank-and-file police officers in legitimating their time and activities to bureaucratic administrators. She thus gained acceptance as a functioning, viable member of the department's rank-and-file patrol squad.

AMRs' greater degree of participation in the group's core activities accords them a higher level of trust and acceptance among setting members than PMRs attain. As a result, they do not have to rely as exclusively on the bonds of friendship they establish with members to generate the rapport and confidence necessary to gather data. AMRs' relationships with setting members may therefore be activity oriented and businesslike, in addition to personal in character.

AMRs generally involve a greater portion of their selves with the setting and its members than do PMRs. This is due to several factors. First, AMRs often share something in common with the people they study. In

Rochford's (1985) study of the Hare Krishnas, for example, he was drawn toward an active membership role partly because he, like they, wanted to explore his spiritual self. In our study of college athletics, Peter shared with the players and coaches an avid interest in sports. This is not to say that AMRs need to be demographically similar to the people they study. While Rochford, as a Caucasian youth in his twenties, had much in common with his subjects, Peter, Jennifer Hunt, and James Marquart (discussed shortly) were rather unlike the people they investigated: Peter was a middle-class white in a group of primarily black athletes and coaches; Hunt was a women in a man's world; and Marquart was an urban, "educated Yankee," surrounded by rural, ill-educated cowboy types. A second reason AMRs identify more closely with their settings is that the activities of the group in which AMRs participate draw them closer to their subjects. During Marquart's (1983, 1985) research on a southern maximum security prison, he was employed as a prison guard. He lived on the premises seven out of every ten days, associated constantly with guards, inmates, and administrators, and had to fulfill the duties of his job. He notes, then, that over the course of his research, he "slowly adopted the guard perspective due to [his] close association and interaction with other guards" (Marquart, 1985: 18).

AMRs' involvement and commitment to their subjects falls short of that experienced by complete participants, however. While they engage in less role pretense than PMRs, they still cling to some of the latter's detachment. As Marquart (1985: 18-19) notes:

> I was a guard and not free from the enormous pressures of occupational socialization. I was expected to think, act, and talk like a guard. It was a personal battle avoiding "going native". . . . Yet three factors helped me adjust and maintain role stability. First, I left the prison on my designated days off. . . . My days off were spent debriefing in my dissertation advisor's office, with friends, and with other faculty members. Maintaining non-guard associations was critical in maintaining my objectivity. Second, I did not derogate or fight inmates for fun. . . . Finally, I made extensive field notes about this role conflict and kept myself aware of how "deep" I was moving into the guard subculture. I knew of this problem and forced myself not to lose all objectivity.

Thus, despite AMRs' functional involvement in their settings, they maintain several escape routes that safeguard their greater commitment to their academic role. First, they periodically withdraw from the setting to nourish their outside interests and limit their involvement (although they cannot do this as easily as PMRs because they have obligations to fulfill within the setting). Second, they periodically realign their perspective with those of outsiders in order to analyze the setting critically (the theoretical stance). Third, they retain sight of the fact that, ultimately, their participation in this research will be temporary in scope, and that their personal and career commitments, unlike their fellow participants, lie elsewhere.

Finally, AMRs, like PMRs, can assume either overt or covert roles in their settings. Their greater involvement in the core activities of the group makes them more likely to use overt approaches since the active membership role is more demanding of their time and selves. They are less likely to feel the need for the secrecy and inconspicuousness associated with the covert role, as their participation and active membership status can generate considerable trust for them among group members.

The Process of Membership

BECOMING AN ACTIVE-MEMBER-RESEARCHER

Fieldworkers may assume active membership roles for a variety of diverse reasons. First, like PMRs, they may be motivated to seek this level of involvement by *epistemological ideals*. They may feel that an active membership approach to field research is necessary in order for researchers to grasp the "subjectively meaningful world of members, rather than the objective analytic accounts of their worlds" (Rochford, 1985: 41). While researchers may come to this conclusion out of their own theoretical convictions, setting members are often vocal in urging them into active membership roles. As Marquart (1985: 4) notes:

> Overall, the guards and convicts were supportive of my efforts to "understand" the prison world. Yet they all voiced the same concern that I should work as a guard and observe the prison "in the trenches"—that from the insider's perspective I could learn more about prisoner control than as a complete outsider.

Rochford (1985: 30) remarks on the reactions of members to researchers once they have assumed an active membership role:

> EBR: . . . I want to write something that allows people to appreciate the devotees from their point of view.
>
> Second Devotee: You should become a devotee.
>
> First Devotee: He *is* a devotee!

Second, fieldworkers may be drawn into active membership roles because of *structural factors* endemic to their settings. In some settings, there are a limited range of roles available, and researchers can only choose from among these select few. Rochford (1985: 26-27) describes the types of research roles he discovered shortly after he entered the Hare Krishna community:

> There had been little differentiation in the types of members in ISKCON; one was either an insider (a devotee) or an outsider (a karmie). . . . Other kinds of members were not recognized. . . . The exclusivist structure of the movement

made it nearly impossible for less committed persons to find an acceptable role within the community.

During Rochford's initial encounters with the devotees, he had hoped to be able to establish himself as a researcher rather than as a potential convert. His initial aspirations were to remain a "strict observer" rather than to become a "quasi-participant." After some time, however, the conflict between his desired role and what could be tolerated by the members came to a crisis point and he was forced to make a decision:

> In the morning, when all the devotees were chanting their rounds in the temple, I refrained from doing so. . . . I observed for a while, but then realized that I was being observed more than I was observing. . . . I felt that I was being avoided (looked down upon) because of my refusal to take part in the chanting. I started wishing that I was somewhere else—anywhere. I had visions of the study coming apart at the seams. . . . At this point I felt I had better take the beads and try chanting. I succumbed to the pressure [Rochford, 1985: 24].

He became an active member, then, out of situational necessity rather than epistemological preference. In discussing how situational necessity can propel researchers into active membership roles, Hunt (1985) notes that "when I ran in for the knife fight, I did so not because I was brave or wanted involvement, but because it concerned life (mine and the rookie's), and action was necessary."

Settings that relentlessly press researchers toward core involvement are those characterized by a strong insider/outsider distinction. As discussed in Chapter One, they may use various "dynamics of inclusion" (Emerson and Pollner, 1983), including inducting researchers into instrumental tasks, trying to recruit them into full membership, and seeking to establish greater intimacy than a strictly research role would entail.

A third factor influencing researchers to assume active membership roles is rooted in their own *personal characteristics*. There are instances in which researchers, for reasons involving themselves as individuals, can get the entrée and perspective on the setting they are studying only if they take an active membership stance. In Hunt's study, for example, the inner dynamics of the setting were primarily limited to the view of male members. Had she acquiesced and assumed one of the members' categories of gender available to her ("dyke," "whore," or "management [office] cop"), she would have gained no more than a marginal role. She would never have attained the confidence of either her "street cop" or her higher-ranking officer respondents because they would have seen her as either too "dirty" or too "clean" to be trusted. She therefore had to carve out an active role that was "liminal" in its character, falling in between the margins of the recognized categories, rules, groups, and structures. Only by continuous, conscious efforts to show the cops that she acted and thought as they was she able to overcome her gender and status barriers and achieve the role of "street-woman-researcher."

Researchers enter into active membership roles via one of two routes: They either *step up their involvement* from earlier insider or peripheral membership roles or *enter directly* into active membership roles. By far the most common route is the former. This corresponds to the way people become involved with groups, organizations, and social movements, more generally, in naturally occurring social interaction. Three of our four examples for this chapter moved through insider, peripheral member roles on their way to active membership. Marquart worked as a research assistant on a project evaluating the Texas Department of Corrections for a summer, and then conducted participant observation on his own. At the prison, he studied for a year and a half before he applied for a job as a guard there. Peter, as noted in Chapter 2, operated in a peripheral role for a year before he became more involved in the team's daily operations. Rochford interacted as an uncommitted observer for several months before he was persuaded to adopt the role of devotee. Later, he became even more deeply involved, taking on a more participatory character (he identified himself in the movement to a greater degree and worked in its elementary school). Hunt, in contrast, entered the setting at an active membership level, having the prior intention of studying it. She had been hired as a researcher by a consultant firm that was engaged to evaluate and compare the performance of male and female rookies. Although she worked as a field observer on a study of New York police officers for a year, she did not have previous contact with the department she evaluated. Field researchers who move immediately into active membership roles are thus likely to be those who join a group for the purpose of studying them, or those who find themselves in a setting where they function as members (i.e., people who first take a job somewhere).

A final dimension associated with becoming an AMR concerns the researcher's degree of input in creating that role. A spectrum exists here between AMRs who *assume an existing role* in the setting (albeit with minor modifications) versus those who *forge a role* for the purpose of doing research. While it may be beyond the researchers' choice as to whether they can create their ideal research role (some settings are not that flexible), their perspective may still be influenced by the degree to which their role is an established or innovated one. Our examples in this chapter span the continuum between these two poles. Marquart, by working as a prison guard, fitted himself into an established role, although he broadened it with his research interests. Unlike the other cases, he shared the activities, quarters, and position of a group of people in the setting. On the other hand, Peter, by creating a position on the team that had never existed and that was tailored to his specific talents (interpersonal, academic, career counseling), falls at the other end of the spectrum. He functioned as a loner, treading a tightrope of trust between the various groups in the setting, whose interests often conflicted with each other. Rochford and Hunt fall at mid-levels along the spectrum. Both engaged in some of the same activities as setting members, since their roles incorporated a combination of assumed and innovated roles, and both were formally focused around membership research.

THE MEMBERSHIP EXPERIENCE

The membership experience of AMRs differs substantially from that of PMRs. One of the primary differences stems from the nature of the *research exchange*. In taking an active membership role, researchers assume a greater degree of formally defined involvement, participation, and commitment. Researchers contribute to the setting and its members through the specified activities of their positions. Rather than constantly searching for informal, unstructured places where they can contribute to securing and maintaining their entrée and rapport, the active membership experience is characterized by more stability. For instance, when Peter took an active membership role by becoming an assistant coach, he no longer had to strain to invent ongoing ways of compensating for their research assistance and openness, but could channel his efforts into the avenue he had formally negotiated with the team.

The *role demands* placed on AMRs are greater than those generally encountered by PMRs. AMRs are expected to behave like full-fledged members in many respects. This includes making repeated displays of involvement and commitment to the group. When these are not forthcoming, members make it clear that the role demands have been violated. This happened to Peter during the course of the college athlete research. As a professor who was both a "friend of the program" and a member of the coaching staff, he was expected to give "decent" grades to the athletes in his classes. This conflicted with his professorial role obligation not to jeopardize his academic integrity by giving grades away. He was usually able to resolve these two sets of demands by working with the athletes in his classes during special tutoring sessions to make sure they learned the material and completed their assignments. When this was not adequate, however, some players did receive failing grades. This caused a breach in the expectation many members of the program had for him. Considerable work was required to mend this violation of trust, and, in fact, in some cases, the severence was never fully repaired.

AMRs are also expected to fulfill their membership role demands in interacting with outsiders. This includes serving as faithful lieutenants and acting on behalf of the group in an appropriate manner. The transition to active membership status affected Peter's interactions with fans, boosters, and the media:

> No longer was I being asked for my personal opinion; I was now being asked as a representative of the team. . . . Defending the faith became a frustrating obligation of my new role as member. . . . This required holding back my

actual feelings, offering carefully measured "party lines," and speaking nicely to people who were rude [Adler, 1984: 318].

Marquart found that his membership role demands included maintaining silence about numerous acts of violence that he witnessed and in which he was occasionally called upon to participate. These included incidents where guards illegally beat inmates and where he helped other guards restrain inmates while medics sutured their wounds without an anesthetic. Hunt found that her respondents "tested" her allegiance and willingness to give the straight party line by questioning her about her previous research on police in another setting.

These role demands extend to analyzing the findings and writing the data into an article, research report, or book. Respondents expect AMRs to portray their group sympathetically. When Rochford traveled to Krishna communities outside his home base, the letter of introduction he carried made explicit the members' expectations of how he would present the movement:

Burke has been formally associated with the *New Dwarka* community for about five years, chants sporadically, attends temple functions, and performs service. . . . Given this level of involvement, his approach to studying ISKCON goes a little deeper than that done by other "outsiders." His thesis could potentially be published and help to present ISKCON in a favorable light to the public. Kindly, therefore, cooperate with his efforts [Rochford, 1985: 29-30].

Fulfilling this role demand is often problematic, as the process of analysis involves focusing a critical or multiperspectival lens on the group and examining them from a theoretic stance. Rochford found that when he took his findings back to the field, the Krishnas he studied were greatly displeased with what he had written. Their intense feelings that he had violated his membership role obligations by depicting them negatively led them to ostracize him, and to try to discredit him and his work in both the Krishna and academic communities. Hunt's experience in showing her subjects potentially compromising reports of their behavior met with a different response. They liked her articles and agreed to let negative portrayals stand. Hunt (1985) suggests that the response of subjects to unfavorable material varies, and that what is often more important to respondents is that researchers stick to the original bargain they had arranged in negotiating entrée or rapport.

The character of the *membership relations* AMRs experience as a result of their participation in the core activities of the group further distinguishes this role from peripheral membership. As mentioned earlier, AMRs no longer need to rely on friendship as the exclusive basis of their entrée and rapport with group members. Although they continue to develop and maintain deep and meaningful relationships with key informants, their relations with other setting members may be less friendly and more collegial than those of PMRs. In fact, as Peter shifted from a peripheral to an active membership role, his relations with specific individuals also exhibited this shift in character. In a way, he was freed from having to cultivate them personally by being granted active membership status by the most critical gatekeeper, the head coach.

In a less intimate and more bureaucratic setting, the sponsorship of a gatekeeper may not be enough to ensure adequate research relations. Marquart, for instance, was assisted to his job as a prison guard by the warden, yet he was mistrusted by many people because of his suspicious behavior at early phases of the project (taking photographs and asking too many questions). He had to prove himself to be both worthy of his job and personally trustworthy before he could develop the trust of his informants. Hunt's situation was even more difficult because the very people who had facilitated her entry into the setting tried to bias her findings and sabotage her research. By insinuating that she was a spy and not to be trusted, the police department's elite administration sought to limit her access to information they perceived to be potentially damaging to their court case. The hostile nature of her relations with these gatekeepers made her have to work even harder to establish trust, yet ultimately their stance toward her backfired against them. Set against the background of tremendous conflict between the elite and the rank and file, her harassment by the elite helped to cement her relations with rank-and-file officers in the long run. She notes:

> I recall several men who were talking about how the brass would love to get something on the "girls" (the policewomen, to get rid of them). Then they both looked at me and added, "they'd like to get something on you too" [Hunt, 1985].

In establishing relations with members of the setting, Hunt drew a firm line between collegial relations and personal ones. She avoided fraternizing after work or becoming intimate with setting members lest that cast an unwanted dimension onto her role. Like Horowitz, she found that the wrong kind of closeness (i.e., sexual) can be damaging to research relations in certain situations. Unlike Horowitz, however, she was able to prevent this problem from developing.

Finally, in establishing membership relations, AMRs must deal with the differences between the life goals of their subjects and themselves. While PMRs are thrust into intimate personal relationships with people they study, AMRs' relationships with such individuals are likely to be augmented (or supplanted) by the close sharing of occupational experiences and concerns (such as reacting under fire to life-and-death situations). However, although AMRs' immediate involvement in the group may overlap with their subjects, their longer-term plans are usually quite different from most members. Here, like PMRs, it is incumbent upon researchers to understand the members' subjective point of view, as much as possible. Of our examples, Peter was the most different from his subjects and had to make the biggest personal leap to understand basketball players' "tunnelvision" on the immediate demands and rewards of their athletic role at the expense of their academic careers. At the other end, Rochford encountered little or no such gap to bridge. The main difference between the full members and himself lay in their greater degree of commitment to the spiritual mission inherent in the movement and their willingness to make sacrifices on its behalf. He therefore diverged from them in the prioritization more than the content of his life goals, and in the methods he deemed appropriate to achieve these goals.

Like PMRs, AMRs become involved in various webs of *membership affiliations*. Just as PMRs are drawn into alliances or perceived connections with some members of the setting more strongly than others, AMRs are prone to affiliation with those involved in participatory roles similar to their own. In some cases, these affiliations precede researchers' becoming involved in active membership roles and help them to achieve this status. In other cases, the affiliations develop out of researchers' type and degree of participation in the group. The particular web of affiliations each researcher forms varies with his or her type of active membership role. In Peter's case he sought to diminish excessive affiliation with any group exclusively, and tried to maintain a neutral position in between all the parties involved in the setting. He listened to the coaches' problems, gave them advice, and aided them in achieving some of their goals. He also did the same for the players, the athletic administrators, and the academic administrators. He often tried, in fact, to mediate problems and conflicts between individuals from these different groups. While this gave him access to the perspective of all groups, it entailed considerable strain and effort.

For Marquart, the membership affiliation was considerably more localized. His employment as a guard placed him squarely within the midst of this group and its subculture. He then faced the more classic problem of overcoming difficulties in gathering data on other parties in the setting. Through his guard sponsorship and good reputation, he managed to make fairly good inroads with the elite inmates, those who occupied positions of power and status within the inmate social system, but as he indicates:

> Although I cultivated a number of inmate elite informants, I had great difficulty in interviewing the "run of the mill" inmates. My uniform was a barrier and limited my access to those prisoners and I was never able to completely resolve this problem [Marquart, 1985: 20].

Rochford's experiences with membership affiliation were still different. Although he resisted at first, he ultimately became a participating, partially committed group member. During the course of his research, however, the Krishnas became divided over the issue of goals and survival. They moved away from the practice of distributing books and soliciting donations toward "picking" (selling products) as a primary source of income. His membership feelings about the proper direction for the movement led him to join a splinter group of Krishnas who were critical of this new trend. This membership affiliation was then used against him when the dominant group of Krishnas attempted to discredit his work. They cited his association with this splinter faction and claimed that his findings represented the perspective of this dissatisfied arm rather than the group as a whole.

A final dimension of AMRs' membership experience lies in the *changes and shifts* researchers encounter within the role. First, every active membership role has a natural history or career. Within even the most preexistent assumed role, there comes a time when the researcher must personalize it and let his or her self emerge. This process of role making, as opposed to mere role taking, extends or expands the role in the direction the researcher desires. Growing in a research role is one of the most enjoyable and creative parts of the data-gathering process, for it accompanies the development of a more secure foundation of trust within the setting.

After the AMR has become more confident and established, and has gathered considerable data, he or she usually begins to feel at home in the setting. Participating in the core activities of members can lead researchers to, inadvertently, change their original feelings toward the group. Their initial balance of involvement and detachment may shift, propelling them toward greater commitment. Rochford (1985: 33-34) indicates how this happened to him:

> While it was necessary to find an acceptable role within the Los Angeles community (not as a researcher, but as a participant) in order to develop the relationships necessary to conduct the research, these very relationships served to socialize me into ISKCON and Krishna Consciousness. From my earliest stance of avoiding participation at all costs, my position within the community developed into one in which I took on the status of a member. The task of adequately attending to both roles often produced difficulties for the research itself, and it also created personal dilemmas for me about what my involvement meant, both to me personally and to the persons who knew me apart from the movement.

In an extreme form, this growth of personal involvement can lead researchers to go native in the setting. They may become swept up in the practical concerns and activities of the setting and forget about explicitly gathering data. They may become so enmeshed in the perspectives of members that they cannot step outside of them. One of Rochford's friends leveled this charge at him, saying:

> I could see the way that you were getting involved actually was skewing the way that you were interpreting what was going on. I just felt that it was increasingly difficult for you to be, not objective, but just critical [Rochford, 1985: 35].

In contrast to complete-member-researchers, for whom going native is a more integral part of their research experience and role, AMRs who attain this level of involvement usually do so for only a fairly limited time. They immerse themselves completely (although generally not intentionally) within the full membership experience and then withdraw. While this can lead to some of the negative effects noted by traditional field researchers, such as adopting members' taken-for-granted perspectives toward occurrences in the field, this can also serve as a positive occurrence. Active membership brings researchers, even if only temporarily, into the members' first-order perspective. This leads them to penetrate beyond a rational to an irrational, emotional, and deep understanding of the people and setting they are studying. By temporarily losing themselves in the natural attitude of members and abandoning the theoretic stance they come closer to making these worlds their own rather than ceding them as others'.

The experience of going native, or gaining commitment, may also occur on a less intense scale to researchers who do not completely lose sight of their outside perspective. As William James (1890) first noted, this membership role becomes another one of the individual's social selves, as much an integral part of his or her composite being as any other self.

While experiencing this level of commitment, AMRs may develop a personal interest or stake in the setting and the activities of its members. They may grow frustrated by what they see, or become emboldened and try to influence the behavior of either individuals or the collectivity. Peter did this when he tried to "protect" college athletes from being exploited by various parties (including themselves) and help them build toward postathletic careers. Rochford did this by taking a political stance within the movement and trying to preserve the "integrity" of what he perceived as its founder's original ideals. Ironically, the futility of both their endeavors served to show them the strength and sources of power supporting the conditions they tried to "ameliorate."

Hunt's experience in taking a stance in her setting was more successful in its outcome. She became personally involved in the efforts of the policewomen under evaluation to prove themselves and to resist the political efforts of the administration to drive them off the force. She attended secret strategic planning meetings held by women officers, spoke forcefully about the politics surrounding the evaluation at pretrial negotiations between the ACLU and the Justice Department, and ultimately, along with two other consultants, secretly hired an attorney who threatened legal action if the police administration, the city, or the consulting firm further interfered with the evaluation. Ultimately, the elite administration lost the court battle and its prominent members resigned from the department (Hunt, 1985).

Another common phase in the career of an AMR is the experience of discontent. AMRs who remain in their settings long enough to take a stance often alienate some respondents or become discontented with the setting. Both Rochford and Hunt created hostility toward themselves through their partisan positions.

Peter and Rochford developed their own feelings of discontent, or ambivalence, which were instrumental in affecting their decisions to withdraw from their settings. In Peter's case, at the same time as his school was changing by becoming more demanding academically, the basketball program was rising in the national rankings and feeling more pressure to recruit good players regardless of their academic ability. He, among others, was one of the principal persons to feel the crunch of this increasingly irresolvable conflict. Rather than being placed in a position where he would have to jeopardize his academic integrity, as he perceived that the other coaches did, he resigned his position. He, like Rochford, became troubled and discontented by the "fade of idealism" he perceived in his setting. While they both recognized this, sociologically, as a common and sometimes inevitable pragmatic response to the structural conditions of life, they chose, and had the luxury of being able, to terminate their active membership roles.

DISENGAGEMENT

In contrast to a peripheral membership role, where researchers can slip away with a modicum of difficulty, it is more problematic for AMRs to disengage from their research roles. For one thing, the functional role they fill in the setting may need to be replaced by another person. One of Peter's tasks before leaving, in fact, was to institute and shape a search for a new academic adviser who would partially re-create the efforts he had made on behalf of the team, despite the fact that this position had not existed before his arrival.

Members of the setting may also be loath to relinquish someone whom they view as a member or quasi member. David Snow, for example, who took an active membership role in his study of a Nichiren Shosnu Buddhist group, notes that his first signs of disengagement were met with a flurry of reconversion activity (Snow, 1980: 110):

No sooner had I finished (telling my group leader about my growing disillusionment) then he congratulated me, indicating that (such feelings) were good signs. He went on to suggest that . . . something is really happening in my life. . . . Rather than getting discouraged and giving up, I was told to participate even more. He also suggested that I should go to the Community Center at 10:00 this evening and get further guidance from the senior leaders. . . . Later in the evening my group leader stopped by the apartment at 10:00—unannounced—to pick me up and rush me to the Community Center to make sure that I received "guidance."

While I was thus trying to curtail my involvment and offer what seemed to be legitimate reasons for dropping out, I was yet being drawn back at the same time.

This institutional "clinging" to researchers is especially prevalent in groups whose mission is to actively convert new members.

A third factor hampering the disengagement of AMRs lies in the personal ties they have formed with members of the setting. Like PMRs, AMRs establish strong and intimate friendships with the people they study, especially their key informants. While disengaging from their active membership roles does not mean that researchers will cut themselves off from their close friends in the setting, it does lead to a change in these relationships. Researchers who disengage are not around as much, do not do the same things they did for their friends (help them out, provide moral support, keep them company), and, ultimately, do not see them as much. Despite the best intentions on both sides, their relationship often erodes. After Peter disengaged from his role as an assistant coach and ceased to hang around the team as much or to assist players with their schedules and problems, several members expressed to him their strong feelings of abandonment.

Not all disengagements are met with negativity and resentment, however. In some cases, researchers are given warm send-offs when they quit their role. Marquart, for example, describes his subjects' reactions upon his departure, and his interpretation of it:

> On my last day of work, the officers gave me an inmate-made card with signatures of many officers and inmates and a plaque containing a cell block key and inscription. From my close inmate contacts, I received three new belts, a holster, two wallets, a notepad holder, and one inmate gave me his "favorite" knife. These gifts produced an emotional high for me. In the eyes of the officers and inmates I had succeeded in the drama of prison life [Marquart, 1985: 16].

This supportive type of treatment is most often received by researchers who let external considerations guide their departure from the field (time constraints, other obligations, and so on) rather than staying for an indefinite period and disengaging when factors internal to the setting demand it.

Positive disengagements are also more likely to occur when researchers make an *abrupt* rather than gradual withdrawal. When researchers depart abruptly, even if this is preannounced, it suggests that they are leaving because they have other pressing business toward which they must turn their attention. Respondents generally accept this rationale without feeling bitter. Researchers who fade out gradually, however, give respondents a sense that they could remain in the setting on a longer and more involved basis, but that they have intentionally chosen not to do so, and that something in the setting has caused them to want to leave. This creates greater feelings of resentment among respondents at the same time that their relationship with the researcher is changing.

Disengagement can take several forms. First, the AMR can withdraw to a peripheral membership role. Peter did this when he resigned his position as assistant coach and gave up his intensive involvement in managing the academic careers of college athletes. Instead of leaving the setting altogether, he continued to hang around occasionally, on a more informal basis. He moved from his bench seat during games to the second row, and still dropped by the athletic offices and gym for talks with the players and coaches. But his relationship with members was somewhat strained by the memory of what it had been and their feelings of resentment about his withdrawal. For these reasons, the likelihood of AMRs disengaging to peripheral membership roles is low.

More often, AMRs quit their settings entirely or withdraw to nonmembership roles. In the latter case, they remain in contact with key informants so that they can ask these individuals questions or conduct follow-up interviews with them, as necessary, during the analysis and writing of their data. Depending on their continuing relationship with setting members they may submit what they have written for members to critique, validate, or modify, as Rochford and Hunt did.

The process of disengagement, analysis, organization, and writing of the data may be a difficult one for former AMRs. As Rochford (1985: 39) notes, the contrast between earlier involvement and present detachment coupled with a critical or detached examination of the scene may lead researchers to experience feelings of betrayal:

> After I began analyzing my data and writing the dissertation I avoided attending functions at the temple and more or less dropped out of sight. . . . At first I was afraid that the devotees would ask about the dissertation, what topics I was writing about and so on. Because I increasingly came to see the dissertation taking a more critical line of analysis, I wanted to avoid going into any details. But after several months these feelings gave way to more intense concerns. I felt that the devotees would in all probability feel betrayed by me. After all, many of them had given me open access to their lives primarily because they had seen me as a member and had understood me to be sincere in my feelings toward ISKCON and Krishna Consciousness. Also, by now I was unsure and confused about exactly what my true feelings toward ISKCON and Krishna Consciousness were. If I was a member of any conviction at all, shouldn't I be attending *arati* and other functions at the temple? Had I been lying to myself all this time? Had I really been sincere about my interest in Krishna Consciousness, or had I simply tricked myself into believing that I was for the sake of the research?

These feelings are especially marked among AMRs. PMRs do not experience them because they do not make the same commitment to or involvement with the scene.

Reflections

Assuming an active membership role can have several associated consequences for both the researcher and the researched. One of these involves the relative *legitimacy or stigma* generated by this membership role. Because of AMRs' degree of participation in the activities of the people they study, the legitimacy or stigma they derive from their research activities is likely to be much greater than for PMRs. Once gained, their status also varies with respect to the perceptions of insiders and outsiders.

Outsiders recognize the signs of affiliation achieved and displayed by AMRs, and accord these researchers somewhat greater respect or disdain than they do PMRs. For Peter, this partly took the form of greater legitimacy for both his association with the team and his research (there was a formal purpose for his hanging around with the team; he wasn't just "sniffing jock straps"). At the same time, however, it also generated greater stigma than had his previous peripheral membership role. Members of his university community became aware of his formal connection to the athletic program and he was subjected to the antiathletic snobbery, suspicion, and resentment of academic elitists. He was eventually told by his department chair that unless he removed himself from his research setting his tenure would be in "serious jeopardy." The stigma Rochford experienced among friends, colleagues, and university administrators was even more intense. He was accused of going native in the setting and his every act was scrutinized as a symbol of his degree of personal involvement in the movement: his dress, his expressions, his possessions, and his attitudes. He was suspected of being a front for the movement, psychopathological, and some kind of social "creep."

While outsiders are vaguely aware of the difference between a researcher's peripheral or active membership involvement, this distinction is more acutely felt by insiders. Members know the difference between someone who is hanging out in a social or tangential (albeit regular) role and someone who participates directly and functionally in the core features of their activity. Consequently, the status they accord AMRs within the group is considerably higher than that which PMRs can obtain. Thus to the extent that both Marquart and Hunt were able to prove themselves as competent in their roles as prison guard and patrol officer, they were more accepted by members and granted access to quasi-membership status. Similarly, Rochford's recognized status as a devotee was critical to his acceptance by Krishna groups around the country, away from his home research site.

Assuming an active membership role can also have far more profound *effects on the researcher's self* than are generated by peripheral membership involvement. In functioning as a member, researchers get swept up into many of the same experiences as members. While this has the distinct advantage of adding their own selves as data to the research, both as a cross-check against the accounts of others and as a deepened awareness of how members actually think and feel, it propels researchers through various changes. These may be temporary, or they may prove enduring. In our study of college athletes, for example, Peter's association with the team caused him to become a celebrity in his own right. He went from an incognito private citizen to a publicly known figure who was approached by strangers and questioned about the team. He was imputed by the media and consequently by others to be an active force in influencing team performance, as well as an expert who could heal poor play and predict future game outcomes. These experiences and imputations created a new social self for Peter, one he describes as "a self created by the team, media, and audience." The result of his media self being reinforced by so many people was that, despite his doubts, he "came to believe in this new self" (Adler, 1984: 315). Donning this new self affected Peter deeply and personally in several divergent, even opposing, ways:

> The media coverage I received filled me with the conflicting emotions of pleasure and guilt, satisfaction and irritation. It felt great to be placed on the level of the famous sports stars I was studying, to see my name in the paper along with theirs, to watch myself on TV, and to be recognized by strangers in public. . . . It made me feel important to think I was considered worthy of so much media attention.

> But even while I felt myself getting puffed-up, I also knew that my media self was a distortion. . . . The more attention I got, the deeper my private uncertainties grew about whether my actions were producing any of the effects that I was publicly lauded for having accomplished. I felt pangs of embarrassment when outsiders praised the job I was doing. Nagging guilt was always there. Was I getting carried away and letting the media run all over me? Was I exploiting myself for the benefit of others? Was I being exploited? Did my behavior fit my self-image?

> Although I tried very hard to keep my feelings of self-importance in check during the first year of intense media coverage, I found it hard to keep denying that what was presented through the media was "fact." I found the media presentation of myself bigger-than-life, so that despite my efforts to remain rational, I was overcome by feelings of power and importance [Adler, 1984: 320].

Finally, using the active membership role can have distinct *consequences for data gathering*. For Peter, his media-legitimated role focused and identified his membership status with the players and other people we wanted to study. Having an articulated sociological connection to the team made setting members more aware of the interpersonal, social dynamic, and social structural factors that were the focus of our study. As a result, people began to approach him to discuss problems, issues, or thoughts they were having in his "specialty" areas. The data thus came to him in many instances where he would have otherwise had to seek it out, or might never have discovered it.

Rochford (1985: 30-31) further notes that as a result of his membership role, topics of potential research interest both expanded and contracted:

> The devotees were more open and frank about their feelings and observations regarding ISKCON because of my involvement, but they also often omitted talking about certain basic subjects and issues regarding Krishna Con-

sciousness because they saw me as both knowledgeable and committed. For example, when I began researching the movement in the later period for the dissertation, I was never subjected to the recruitment and conversion efforts of devotees, as I had been during my initial phases of research. I was no longer thought of as an inexperienced novice, who had to be taught the fundamentals of the philosophy or convinced of the righteousness of Krishna Consciousness. As a result, in the later period I had little or no access to the dynamics of the recruitment process as it took place interactionally within the community.

The active membership role thus moves researchers into a position where they are able to gain closer, more personal, more accurate, and more in-depth insight into the groups they are studying. This may come at the expense, however, of access to more superficial, marginal, or unintended aspects of the scene.

In comparing this research stance to the classic continuum of field research roles, we find that it corresponds most closely to the definition of the complete participant. Gold (1958: 33) describes the complete participant role as one where the researcher interacts with his subjects "as naturally as possible in whatever areas of their living interest him and are accessible to him as situations in which he can play, or learn to play, requisite day-to-day roles successfully." Researchers can thus join in subjects' occupational or recreational activities under the guise of "pretending to be a colleague." This, then, is a covert role, where researchers alone are aware of their deception and role pretense. Instead of being themselves in their roles, all they can be is their "not selves," reserving their true selves for the observer role they constantly carry suppressed inside themselves as their primary role.

The active membership role involves many of the same types of participation and problems as the complete participant stance. Researchers in both of these postures engage in the same types of activities as members, interacting with them closely. Both AMRs and complete participants feel the pull toward going native, and abandoning themselves to the perspective and posture of the full member. In fact, adopting either of these roles probably requires a certain compatibility of spirit between the researcher and the researched, where researchers become torn in their loyalties between the goals of members and those of academia. Yet both ultimately hold the social science community as their most critical reference point and source of self-identity.

In contrast to the complete participant, however, the AMR does not always assume a covert role in the field. This diminishes the amount of role pretense, although it does not eliminate it entirely. Yet by taking an overt role, as most AMRs do, it enables them to bring more of themselves into their research settings. Rather than being a "not self" in their research role, AMRs imbue all of their roles with some part of their selves. They do not hold back, but use their human selves in forging an integration of what Gold calls "self and role." This is limited by the difference between their and their respondents' values, goals, and commitment to the setting. In sum, AMRs are more distanced from the members than complete participants by the fact that they can take an overt role; they do not have to pretend to be members. But in so doing, AMRs can find greater self-expression in their research roles and integrate their sociological observations with their membership participation.

4. COMPLETE MEMBERSHIP

The complete membership role entails the greatest commitment on the part of the researcher. Rather than experiencing mere participatory involvement, complete-member-researchers (CMRs) immerse themselves fully in the group as "natives." They and their subjects relate to each other as status equals, dedicated to sharing in a common set of experiences, feelings, and goals. As a result, CMRs come closest of all researchers to approximating the emotional stance of the people they study. CMRs' genuine commitment to the group, and the members' awareness of this, diminishes the need for role pretense. In conducting their research, then, CMRs often adopt the overt role.

This description is necessarily ideal typical. In reality, the complete membership role encompasses a range of behaviors that vary along a continuum by the reseachers' degree of commitment to the group and its goals. Progression along the continuum of complete membership is usually associated with researchers relinquishing their involvement in and commitment to their former world and adopting the *weltanschauung*, or worldview, of members. At one end of this spectrum are those researchers who are either incomplete or unsuccessful in fully yielding to the world of members. For example, Barrie Thorne, in her research on the draft resistance movement of the 1960s (Thorne, 1971, 1983), shared the values, beliefs, and goals of other participants, as well as most of their behavior. However, she would not join them in dropping out of school, engaging in activities likely to lead to arrest, or cutting her secure ties to the establishment. On the other end of the continuum are individuals who become so committed to the group that they abandon their ties to the scientific community and fail to return from the field. This happened to Carlos Casteneda during his research on an alternate belief system and reality practiced by a Yaqui Indian whom he called don Juan (Casteneda, 1968, 1971, 1972, 1974, 1977, 1981, 1984).[1] While his initial intention was to collect data about the medicinal plants used by the Indians of the Southwest United States, he uncovered a group of sorcerers and seers. In order to study them he apprenticed himself to the leader, don Juan. Ultimately, however, he became the phenomenon in which he had formerly suspended belief, joining the world of mysterious seers and knowledge he had entered.

For CMRs, commitment is thus the central issue: Have researchers immersed themselves fully in the field as members? How much have they adopted as their own the beliefs, values, and goals of members? To what extent do they identify with the social science community and/or with the setting? How much do they carry with them some element of detachment from the members' world?

In contrast to the two previous research roles, the complete membership role can be divided into two distinct subtypes: the "opportunistic" (Riemer, 1977) researcher and the "convert."[2] In the former, researchers study settings in which they are already members. David Hayano, for example, conducted a study of poker cardrooms in Gardena, California (Hayano, 1982), where he was already established as a regular player. Susan Krieger also conducted an opportunistic study of a midwestern lesbian community (Krieger, 1983, 1985) of which she had been a member for a year. In the latter, researchers "become the phenomenon" they are studying. They select a setting for study in which they are not previously involved, and in conducting the research they become converted to group membership. In Burke Forrest's research on spiritualist groups in Southern California and England (Forrest, 1986, forthcoming), for example, she became inducted into mediumship as a result of her years of training. Benetta Jules-Rosette's study of an African Apostolic church and community (Jules-Rosette, 1975, 1976) also involved a conversion experience. Although she had originally intended to study the interface between African religion and Christian practice from a noncommitted stance, she and her husband both succumbed to the group's proselytizing and became baptized true believers. This convert role of becoming the phenomenon is associated with the ethnomethodological perspective.

As these examples illustrate through their variations in induction, involvement, and commitment, a sliding scale of membership exists even within the complete membership role. Each of the three membership roles we discuss in this book constitute somewhat flexible typological categories. Within a single membership role, then, individuals may vary in their type and degree of participation, depending on the constraints of the setting and their personal or professional preference.

The Process of Membership

The membership experiences of CMRs differ from PMRs' and AMRs' largely by their degree of self-immersion in their settings. In examining this membership process, we will differentiate between the experiences encountered by opportunistic and convert CMRs.

BECOMING A COMPLETE-MEMBER-RESEARCHER

Opportunistic researchers vary from convert researchers most in the origin of their involvement with the research. Riemer (1977) notes that part of the "sociological imagination" involves inward reflection upon researchers' unique historical and biographical experiences. He proposes that using an "opportunistic research strategy" can benefit researchers in their sociological enterprise. Rather than neglecting "at hand" knowledge or expertise, they should turn familiar situations, timely events, or special expertise into objects of study. Individuals who opportunistically exploit their membership in some scene or group by turning their sociological optic upon it fall into this category of CMRs.

Hayano (1979) calls this type of research "auto-ethnography," the cultural study of one's "own people." Differentiating among several categories of auto-ethnographers, he identifies those whose "master status" (Hughes, 1945) is the same as the people they study (such as Cavan, 1972, or Hostetler, 1978), those who have acquired an intimate familiarity with certain subcultural, recreational, or occupational groups (i.e., Polsky, 1969; Mitchell, 1983; Scott, 1968), and those who become formally or informally socialized, after indoctrination, into a specific group's knowledge or way of life (this last category corresponds most closely to our definition of the convert CMR). Uniting these diverse kinds of auto-ethnographies is that,

> in each case, the researchers possess the qualities of often permanent self-identification with a group and full internal membership, as recognized both by themselves and the people of whom they are a part [Hayano, 1979: 100].

For most opportunistic CMRs, then, involvement with and membership in the group they study precedes their decision to turn this into a research subject. Of all the membership roles, opportunistic CMRs are most similar to the people they study. Some are born into the group (i.e., Higgins, 1980), some have worked at various jobs before or during their careers as social scientists (i.e., Becker, 1963), while others find themselves thrust into situations and then turn them to use for this purpose (i.e., Roth, 1963). As Hayano (1979: 100) notes, they are "scholars who have acquired (and then exploited) multiple group membership derived from their own personal interests and backgrounds." Both Krieger, whose lesbianism was a major part of her life and self-identity, and Hayano, who had played poker recurrently throughout his life before becoming engulfed in the world of professional players at the cardrooms, fall into this category.

Having a large area of interests and commitments shared with members facilitates researchers' gaining entrée, but it changes the character of this process. Instead of having to bring their research self to a setting and carve out a membership role, the reverse occurs. Here we see people familiar with a setting having to create the space and character for their research role to emerge. They must look at the setting through a fresh perspective, to develop relationships with people they did not associate with previously, to change the nature of their preexisting relationships, and to become involved with the setting more broadly. This can be difficult, awkward, and heighten the sense of unnaturalness that invariably surrounds the research enterprise.

Augmenting the membership role with the research enterprise can also become confusing and overwhelming. Hayano, for instance, simultaneously had to play the cards that he was dealt, think about the other cards that had already passed through the deck, observe his fellow players to try to interpret what they were holding, look for general categories or typologies of action through which he could organize and analyze the scene, and look for behaviors that constituted specific examples of these types to draw upon in his future writings as examples. Becoming a CMR entails putting considerably more time into the setting, but it also makes this time near-schizophrenic in its frenzied multiple focus. The preexisting membership role undergoes a significant transformation.

In contrast, people who become CMRs through a process of conversion undergo an entirely different experience. The initial interest in the setting is purely data oriented. Their role as a researcher precedes and takes an early priority over their complete membership role. At some point during the course of their involvement in the setting, however, they undergo a conversion experience that sets new priorities for the balance of these roles, increasing the salience of their membership. According to Jules-Rosette (1976: 132-133), conversion as a generic process has three significant features. First, it involves a psychological transformation where the convert's underlying assumptions about the world are reconstructed. Second, it involves a social rite of passage in which the individual makes a socially recognized move from one status and/or social environment to another. Third, it involves the cognitive and emotional surrender of one form of life and the acceptance of another. Conversion, or becoming the phenomenon, thus involves a much more dramatic self-alteration than anything experienced by opportunistic CMRs.

The conversion experience can come about in one of two ways. Researchers can enter the field with the express intention of making a "good faith commitment" to becoming the phenomenon. This can be based on either their epistemological principles, their interest in the group they are studying, or their evaluation of the pragmatic requisites for studying this group. In undertaking a study of African secret societies, for example, Bellman (1984) knew that to get any valid data he had to become an accepted member of the group. Forrest's decision to enroll in training classes at the local spiritualist church, however, was dually motivated by her epistemological commitment "to experience and document the process of becoming a member" (Forrest, forthcoming), and by her sense of the setting as "exciting and fun."

It often happens, however, that researchers who end up becoming the phenomenon begin their research without the prior intention of converting to full membership. For example, Jules-Rosette began her research imbued with "preconceived notions about the objectivity and neutrality of the observer" (1975: 21), and had no intention of pursuing membership. In reflecting afterwards, she characterized her research experience as "a gradual transition from the perspective of a participant observer to that of an observing participant" (1975: 22). When Casteneda asked don Juan to teach him about medicinal plants, he had neither the awareness of the sorcerers' setting he was ultimately to discover nor the desire to commit his whole life to it. It was only in retrospect, after his task had been partially accomplished, that he identified what he had been doing:

> In the case of my work with don Juan I have limited my efforts solely to viewing him as a sorcerer and to acquiring *membership* in his knowledge [Casteneda, 1972: viii; emphasis in original].

During their early experiences in the setting, these researchers generally feel temptations and enticements toward membership. As Weber (1949) notes, the choice of what we study carries an implicit value statement in it, and while future CMRs may not be part of the subcultures they chose to study, they feel an affinity with and curiosity toward them. These may be exploited by people in the setting who want to draw them further into the core. Casteneda was constantly manipulated by don Juan, who whetted his appetite for more information and exposure to this secret world with mysterious allusions and cryptic statements that would be understandable only, it seemed, to one who was more knowledgeable. But knowledge required commitment and a change in life-style; something Casteneda yielded to only gradually.

Accompanying these temptations and enticements are often a variety of pressures toward membership. From the earliest of Jules-Rosette's associations with the Apostolic church, the members conveyed to her their absolute certainty that she had been sent to them for the purpose of bringing their mission to America, where she would open a church. Like any unaffiliated individual associated with an actively proselytizing group, she was urged in many subtle and direct ways to convert.

Despite this, usually unconverted researchers resist making a full commitment to the members' world. While they are tempted to and do move closer to them, they also go through periods where they resist these worlds. Jules-Rosette resisted the members' efforts to convert her for many months; she did not want to renounce her Western beliefs, clothes, and medicines. Forrest clung to her traditional assumptions about the world; she was skeptical of the spiritualists' "alogical" thought. As she notes, this hindered her progress in her spiritualist training:

> Meantime I was having difficulty getting images of any kind whatever. It was a big headache which was complicated by the fact that I had studied enough psychology to know a plethora of words like "hypnagogue" and "eidetic imagery," which, while being descriptive rather than explantory, gave me a comforting sense of being in control [Forrest, forthcoming: 21].

For many years Casteneda also clung to rational explanations of the supernatural phenomena he witnessed. He constructed elaborate accounts to spare himself from squarely facing the knowledge that the world he now encountered was not as he had always imagined it.

The strength of researchers' resistance to full conversion into new groups comes from the fact that, as Jules-Rosette notes, adopting a new form of life often involves surrendering another. The beliefs of the new group may conflict with those previously held by researchers. This is particularly pronounced when researchers study groups exploring alternate or "subjective realities" (Forrest, 1986) such as spiritualism or sorcery, but may be found even in more mundane settings. As researchers follow the path toward membership, they enter and leave these realities each time they foray into the research setting. They experience prolonged cognitive dissonance from the *shock* of trying to deal with these multiple realities. Drawing on Schutz's (1967) discussion of multiple realities, Jules-Rosette (1976: 135) refers to this as a "powerful clash resulting from the shift from one realm of thought and action to another, a moment of specific shock." For Jules-Rosette, who fully immersed herself in her setting for a year, the shock was not as great because the immediate Apostolic reality overwhelmed her. Both Forrest and Casteneda experienced considerable stress, however, due to their intermittent exposure to their research worlds. Casteneda (1974: 45) recounts his feelings after being confronted with an experience his ordinary reality could not explain:

> I felt that I was truthfully cut in two; some part of me was not shocked at all and could accept any of don Juan or don Genaro's acts at their face value. But there was another part of me that flatly refused; it was my strongest part. My conscious assessment was that I had accepted don Juan's sorcery description of the world merely on an intellectual basis, while my body as a whole entity refused it, thus my dilemma.

It is significant to note that this shock phenomenon is not found among opportunistic researchers who are native to the group they study. Such auto-ethnographers have already (perhaps from birth, perhaps from natural inclination) incorporated the essential features and implications of the settings they are studying into their worldview.

Convert members undergo their transition into complete membership differently, some undergoing a sudden transformation, while others progress through a more gradual process of acceptance that is punctuated by various benchmarks of reversal and recommitment. Jules-Rosette's experience involved a continuous progress toward commitment characterized by sudden leaps of illumination and faith, alternating with long, uneventful periods. Casteneda took dramatic plunges deep into membership while he was in a "state of heightened awareness," but when he returned to his normal awareness he would become anxious and withdraw. Forrest eked along at a slower rate, trying to control her degree of involvement in both worlds carefully so that the transition would not prove too traumatic. These diverse experiences illustrate the range in pace, character, and intensity encountered by CMRs in their movement sequence toward conversion. For convert CMRs, this journey may consume the major portion of their stay in the field.

THE MEMBERSHIP EXPERIENCE

The research character of the CMR is in many ways more complex than that experienced by PMRs and AMRs, being marked by extreme intensity yet, at the same time, divided into two types.

The first struggle, which impels CMRs throughout a significant portion of their research, is *role immersion*. For convert researchers, who enter the setting relatively secure in their research role, the focus is on developing the involvement in and commitment to the membership role. We have previously examined various aspects of this process as they pertain to the convert CMR. For opportunistic CMRs the situation is reversed: They begin the research secure in their membership role and must struggle to forge a research role. For Hayano this meant expanding his focus to encompass more aspects of the setting and the multidimensional character of peoples' involvement with it. He had to vary the times and durations of his visits, and begin recording his observations more systematically. For Krieger this involved an even more radical departure from her previous behavior. With three months remaining before she was to move to another town, she decided to undertake a formal study. She turned to her acquaintances, friends, and lovers from this social group and conducted a series of 78 depth interviews with them (the total community). This put her in an awkward position at times, especially when she was dealing with rivals or ex-lovers and attempting to approach them from an uninvolved, value-neutral stance. For her, immersion in the research role was an omnipresent struggle, and one that plagued her well beyond the data-collection phase of the research.

While role immersion represents infusing the self with new dimensions, it also signifies a bifurcation of self. The complete membership role exemplifies the ultimate existential dual role. As a result, in trying to sustain full membership and the research perspective simultaneously, fieldworkers may encounter *role conflict*. This is not always the case, as some researchers find that they can sustain both roles comfortably. Hayano, especially, integrated the research role into his repertoire with minimal difficulty. Jules-Rosette, though, found that the research mind-set had been more compatible with her daily existence as a nonmember participant observer. She describes how this changed after her baptism experience:

> Once the decision to become devoted to Christ and the Spirit was made, conscious reflection on each activity became a hindrance. As an ethnographer, conscious reflection was necessary, and it also was unavoidable for

new members. The ongoing process of conversion was thus characterized by an increasing tension between reflection and participation. I was expected to question just enough to absorb doctrine but not too much [Jules-Rosette, 1976: 157-158].

Undertaking the process of gathering data through the complete membership role thus involves accepting a new role, whether this is the research or the membership role. This may mark the beginning of an extended or infinite period of transition where fieldworkers subscribe to alternate definitions of reality that may not comfortably coexist.

Sometimes it is not the character of the researcher and member roles, but their demands on the researcher that come into conflict. Thorne's research experience was fraught by such "conflicts of consciousness." On the one hand, she felt the need to remain somewhat of a detached, objective, and neutral observer in her research role. Yet her membership role demanded active commitment and involvement. This was a necessary precondition for participation. "At every level the draft resistance movement demanded partisanship. . . . There was no tolerance for neutrality" (Thorne, 1983: 219). Her research experience was thus characterized by a continuous juggling of these two roles and their demands. She made clear the partisan character of her antiwar and antidraft beliefs, and she participated in the routine activities of the two draft resistance groups she was studying (the Boston Draft Resistance Movement—BDRM—and the New England Resistance—NER), but she psychologically distanced herself from these groups by lodging her perspective and ultimate standards of behavior in an outside, comparative framework. This role conflict, and Thorne's refusal to yield to the pressures of full membership, made her feel guilty. She felt as if she was betraying the movement through her dual commitment. The issue of betrayal was one she could not shake, and that came back to haunt her in her relations with members.

The conflict between the beliefs and behavioral demands of being a researcher and being a member can often lead CMRs to experience *role detachment*. Feelings of detachment can be oriented toward one or the other of these roles, and either wax or wane as the research progresses. It is common for convert CMRs to experience detachment from the membership role during the early stages of their research, as they struggle to come close to the phenomenon they are studying. Both Casteneda and Forrest maintained a conscious and rational detachment for years from the otherworldly perceptions and encounters they were having. This gradually diminished as the research evolved, and was replaced by growing feelings of alienation from the research role. The more they became the phenomenon, the greater the difficulty they had focusing a sociological optic on it.

Opportunistic CMRs are more likely to follow the opposing scenario. When caught between the loyalty tugs, behavioral claims, and self-identification dilemmas of the divergent research and membership roles, opportunistic CMRs usually feel initially more closely aligned with their membership status. Their early research endeavors are marked by difficulties in creating and adjusting to the research role. Krieger, for example, felt so detached from her research role that she could not analyze her data for several years. Originally, she thought that she lacked adequate analytic "distance" from the subjects of her study, from her membership role. She eventually came to realize, however, that in trying to be scientific and detached, she had estranged herself from the very personal feelings surrounding not only her membership role but her research role as well. In trying to be disciplined and objective, she had suppressed herself and thereby lost touch with the feelings and insights generated by her research role. Before she could overcome the detachment from her research experience, she had to reimmerse herself in the feelings she had experienced while gathering data, and had to reinterpret the reactions she had formed at the time. Krieger (1985: 320) offers these reflections on the danger of detaching one's self from the research role:

> The great danger of doing injustice to the other does not come about through use of the self, but through lack of use of a full enough self which, concomitantly, produces a stifled, artificial, limited, and unreal knowledge of others.

While some CMRs may be characterized as having a greater detachment from one role in particular, others shift back and forth between these roles, alternately feeling immersed in or detached from both of them. Accompanying this shifting detachment are feelings of disloyalty and betrayal that become temporarily attached to one of these two roles. When researchers encounter these feelings, they often become concerned about imbalance in their research and struggle to re-fuse themselves with their alienated role.

CMRs' involvement in these roles affects their *relations with members*. Because they are often more like the members than are PMRs and AMRs, and because their interest in a commitment to the group is greater, CMRs generally forge deeper relations with setting members than do other fieldworkers. The greater intensity and intimacy of their relations accentuates the multifaceted character of the complete membership role, causing members to be more sensitive to the two dimensions it encompasses. Adding a research aspect onto the relationship or trying to pursue full membership while carrying a research agenda are thus more delicate endeavors than they might be for a less involved researcher.

In relating to members, CMRs often encounter two kinds of difficulties: accepting them and being accepted by them. Convert researchers usually struggle with the former problem. They stand on the outside watching the natives, often being invited to join them as a full member, but hesitating to take the plunge. Jules-Rosette, Casteneda, and Forrest all worked through this process to varying degrees. Generally, they found it easier to befriend the people than to internalize their goals and values, but until they could accomplish the latter they could not fully accept membership. Krieger encountered a different dimension of this issue. While she lived as a member of her community she could associate with and befriend whomever she chose. Upon becoming a CMR, however, she was thrust into a research relationship with all of the community members. Suddenly she found herself face-to-face with individuals she had not known intimately, discussing private aspects of their lives. In some cases she had trouble accepting them, as one of her postinterview assessments shows:

> INTERVIEW #72: M. was the only one to really break down and cry at the time of the interview and want to be held. This scared me—because I did not want to get involved, and did not want her to become dependent on me. . . . I also had the feelings that I invited this, with everyone. Then when I got it, drew back from it. This left me uneasy. Feeling angry (?), lonely. What if it were me who wanted to cry and be held? [Krieger, 1985: 314]

Yet at the same time, Krieger also struggled with the opposite problem: being accepted by members. A pervasive theme that echoes through her interview self-assessments is the fear of rejection and the desire to be accepted by her respondents:

> INTERVIEW #54: In her office . . . I felt that she was trying to impress me with herself, that I was mostly a pawn to this, a person to be won over, not an independent person to be related to—one who had sensitivity, specialness, etc. and I wanted this other response from her. . . . I wanted to be an equal, a real person to her. I left disappointed [Krieger, 1985: 316].

The struggle to become accepted by members is a relational problem that, ironically, characterizes opportunistic CMRs. Even though they are committed to the group from the onset of the research, the new dimension of their relationship to members and/or their new outside interests set them apart from ordinary members. To the extent that they can disguise this, as Hayano did, or to the extent that members are fundamentally self-interested, as his subjects were, this is less problematic. When the group is highly sensitive about its membership, and when it is formed for the purpose of pursuing a specific goal, the members may resent or even reject the CMR and his/her dual commitment. This was the situation Thorne encountered.

Because of their quasi-legal activities and counterestablishment status, the members of both groups Thorne studied became concerned about government agents infiltrating and spying on them. She notes that, "A common ritual around backstage Resistance gatherings was to play a sort of guessing game: Who's the Fed?" (1983: 227). After a while, members began to resent her attempt to straddle both groups (the BDRM and the NER). This, coupled with her attachment to an outside, social science community, made her a likely focus for suspicion. She was given the cold shoulder, excluded from the collectivity, and, most especially, left out of the "who's the Fed?" rituals. This growing erosion of her acceptance was the direct result of the research-oriented facets of her behavior.

Two distinct aspects of complete membership, as contrasted to that of peripheral and active membership, are the *role expectations and exchanges* inherent in this research relationship. Unlike those other two, where researchers are expected to contribute something to members via their outside or academic role, this emphasis is considerably diminished for CMRs. They are less frequently exhorted to present the group favorably, or to keep the group's secrets; perhaps it is thought that as members they will share these interests with the group. Rather, they are expected to fill the full role of members. It is on this basis that they are primarily treated. This is both an aid and a hindrance to researchers, for while it draws them into the group and allows them to discover the inner features of membership, it inhibits their other interests and commitments, which include their research. Casteneda, for example, was advised by don Juan to "erase his personal history," to detach himself from family members and old friends who knew him well, and to create a fog around himself. In that way he would free himself from the encumbering thoughts of other people, achieve the ultimate freedom of being unknown, and take the first great step along the warriors' path to knowledge and freedom (Casteneda, 1972: 11-17). In so doing, however, he would also be abandoning his outside allegiances and undertaking the beginning of his great transformation and commitment to don Juan's world.

The nature of the exchange, then, is that CMRs yield themselves to the group by making a full commitment of their selves. In return, they are given considerable latitude. Forrest's spiritualist mediums, for example, did not care if she tape recorded or took notes on their seances. They believed, and all that mattered to them was that she had been sent by friendly spirits. Similarly, don Juan did not care that Casteneda was seeking a "key informant" for his anthropological study when he encountered him. To don Juan, power brought Casteneda to him to serve as his apprentice and follow in his footsteps. And though numerous people involved in sorcery and knowledge communicated with Casteneda, urging him to censor or cease his public writings, don Juan never made any such demands. Complete membership role expectations and exchanges are thus fewer, but more profound.

Like PMRs and the AMRs, CMRs become lodged and enmeshed in a network of *membership affiliations*. These friendship and research ties can vary in character from openness to restrictiveness. Hayano and Forrest illustrate examples of the former, as they both roamed fairly free. While they each had their circle of friends with whom they generally "hung out," they were not particularly restricted in their movement or access. Hayano participated in the action at all six Gardena cardrooms at one time or another, went with people to Las Vegas, the track, and other gambling spots, and played at all the tables. During Forrest's California years, her circle of friends change constantly each time someone dropped out of the scene or was moved to a more advanced class. She then re-created this fluidity on another continent in moving to her new setting.

In contrast, other CMRs become embedded in their network affiliations, so that while it reveals things, it also entraps them. In Jules-Rosette's case, she had made the decision to reside with one group of Apostles because of the practical and financial difficulties associated with traveling among the different groups. This brought her in touch with the intensity and character of living within such a group, but it effectively limited the parameters of her study to only that group.

Furthermore, researchers may have modified restriction or access to the full range of membership. This was the case for Thorne, who was able to negotiate membership in two groups, but paid a price for it. She had access to a multiperspectival stance, but her overextension and lack of commitment damaged her relations with many members.

Finally, CMRs are likely to find that their associations with various individuals or groups in the setting will influence their relations with others whom they encounter, affecting the character of the data they can gather from them. Krieger's community, for example, was riddled with networks of past and present friendships and sexual liaisons. As she strove to negotiate her way through the group, she found that many of her own affiliations entered into the research relationships she was attempting to forge with members.

CMRs also resemble PMRs and AMRs in effecting *changes and shifts* over the course of their involvement in their role. Two basic patterns can be discerned. The first, role stability, is mostly characteristic of opportunistic CMRs. Hayano, Krieger, and Thorne all held established roles early in the research and did little to change their involvement over the course of the study. Rather, they moved progressively outward through their settings, systematically broadening their range of focus from the relatively narrow member's vision to the more encompassing scan desired by the CMR.

The second pattern, role identification, is mostly characteristic of convert CMRs. Jules-Rosette, Casteneda, and Forrest all followed a path that led progressively inward toward the central depths of the setting. They may have started out with the intentions of gathering breadth knowledge, but they ultimately became focused on studying their own progression into the core of the group as a means of understanding the setting. As they got closer to becoming the phenomenon they were studying, their experience and understanding of it changed, moving from the intellectual to the visceral. The complete membership role is thus an active one, wherein researchers shift their involvement in different ways in an effort to gain greater knowledge of the setting in its entirety.

DISENGAGEMENT

As with other membership roles, most CMRs must decide, at some point, to draw their research to a close. Due to the intensity of their involvement with and commitment to the setting, this is not necessarily associated with leaving the field. Depending on their inclination and circumstances, some CMRs maintain involvment with their settings and fellow members. Opportunistic CMRs may decide to bring their formal research to a close after they have gained a researcher's understanding of the broad ranges of their settings. However, the very features that served to bring them to the group often lead them to maintain a lifelong interest and involvement in the setting. Such was the case with Hayano, who tapered but never severed his involvement with the cardrooms.

Convert CMRs, in comparison to opportunistic CMRs, are less likely to remain in their settings once the reseach is completed, but more likely to than PMRs and AMRs. In conducting their research they may open up a world that always intrigued them, but which they never made the time or effort to discover. Their research experience may serve as a mode of entrée into an area that will remain a lifelong interest. Their experiences in the field may also change them in some way, such that they do not want to go back to being the way they were before. They may stay in the field, or make frequent visits back to the field, while retaining their commitment to the group or world they studied.

CMRs who do not maintain a continuing affiliation with their settings generally *withdraw* from the field. Once researchers have attained the role of complete members they, like PMRs and AMRs, rarely diminish their involvement to a lesser membership role. They therefore leave the scene. Like PMRs and AMRs, they usually form friendships, especially with key informants, that are lasting. Through these people they can maintain contact with the group for several purposes, including follow-up research and future reentry.

CMRs may leave their settings for several reasons. First, there may be artificial constraints beyond their control that impinge on their ability to remain in the field. Krieger, for example, began her study knowing she would be moving out of town after three months. Jules-Rosette left the setting when her sabbatical leave expired, although there were points during the study when she thought she might not return to the West. Money and time serve as the two main constraints that pull CMRs out of the field against their own volition.

Second, CMRs may leave the field because of the dissolution of the scene. This is one of the main factors causing opportunistic CMRs to detach from settings in which they are engaged. Thorne left the field for this reason. As the draft resistance movement came to a natural conclusion, her two groups disbanded. Studies of social movements are most likely to encounter this form of termination.

Third, some CMRs withdraw from their settings because they have reached their personal limits. As a convert CMR they reach a point where they can proceed no deeper into the setting. This may be due to the increasing difficulty they encounter in handling a set of conflicting realities, or to the fear their setting generates within them. Both Forrest and Casteneda had recurrent bouts of fear, causing multiple withdrawals from their settings. During the latter's apprenticeship with don Juan, there was a three-year period when he cut off all contact with his mentor and vowed never to see him again; don Juan's teachings had begun to pose too serious a threat to his "idea of the world" (Casteneda, 1971: 17). While he ultimately returned to conclude his apprenticeship, Forrest did not. She withdrew twice from her setting, once temporarily, and once permanently. These withdrawals were both caused by her progressing in the setting, being frightened by what she experienced, and either rationalizing it as a trick or being unable to cope with it. Her second, final, withdrawal occurred in London. After a series of vivid apparitions that frightened her, she began to have difficulty eating. She was beginning to feel "crazy." When she went to see a doctor, he told her that if she did not leave the setting she would be "dictating her thesis from a box." She lasted in the setting for two more weeks, but finally left on the verge of emaciation.

Opportunistic CMRs may also reach a point where they encounter their personal limits of involvement in the setting. When fieldworkers transform an arena where they have personal, everyday interest into a focus of study, the character of the setting changes for them. They no longer behave naturally, as they would if they had no ulterior motive. They may become alienated, burned out, or encounter dimensions of the setting that they find excessively distasteful.

Upon leaving the field, CMRs may encounter difficulties in the *analysis and/or writing* of their data. CMRs go beyond acting out the peripheral or core behaviors of the group; they believe in what they are doing. Of all the roles, this is the most highly charged with subjectivity and emotion. When the time finally arrives to immerse themselves purely in the theoretical stance and to commit their analyses to paper, they may encounter serious problems. Krieger found her difficulties in trying to wrest something sociological to say out of 400 pages of rich interview notes as monumental as they were incomprehensible. She stared at, picked up, put down, made copies of, and took notes on these notes for well over a year with no success. Then, in frustration, she gave up, closed the notebooks, and wrote a novel (Krieger, 1985).

Forrest also went for several years after leaving the field without being able to analyze or write about her research experiences. Although this was partly a result of the shock and fear she experienced, there were two other factors preventing her. First, she needed time, to reorient herself slowly to everyday life reality. She refers to this period as "the return to objectivity," writing:

> Both anthropologists and sociologists have written of their problems and experiences in shifting gears upon returning to their own culture or belief system, and how they dealt with the discovery that they themselves had changed in the process of their work. . . . I had to come to terms with the obvious fact that I had entered more deeply in the hidden world than I had supposed [Forrest, 1986: 447-448].

Second, she experienced a profound sense of betrayal. CMRs have such a strong commitment to and self-identification with the group they study that they have an especially hard time portraying them in the light of the detached analyst. They do not want to reveal the members' secrets and foibles, to hurt them in any way, or (most especially) to show them that they thought of them in any way other than the way members think. Nearly all of these, though, must be done if the CMR is to write a theoretical analysis. The final road, then, is particularly difficult for the CMR.

Reflections

Like the peripheral and active, the complete membership role brings to researchers a certain amount of *legitimacy and/or stigma*. Compared to those other membership stances, this one incorporates the greatest, most intense role status, whether in the positive or negative form. Unlike researchers pursuing the previous roles, CMRs have the full acceptance of insiders. For example, Krieger's research on lesbians, a population characterized by living in hidden and secretive worlds (Ponse, 1976), was enormously facilitated by her complete membership status. With outsiders, CMRs also have the full acknowledgment of membership and carry the resulting positive or negative connotation of their associations. In this way they share the experience of AMRs, but not PMRs. CMRs carry an additional stigma in the eyes of outsiders beyond the contagion of their research subjects' status, however. Because they involve and commit themselves fully to the members' world, CMRs encounter, from both lay outsiders and, most especially, other academics, the special stigma associated with going native in a research setting.

A second consequence of the complete membership role lies in its *effects on data gathering*. While researchers may sacrifice some detachment, the depth of the data gathered via this role is a valuable compensation. CMRs are able to gain the full openness of their subjects to an extent unknown by any other kind of fieldworker. This is the result of being fully accepted by members. Krieger, thus, was privy to frank and rich discussions of a highly personal, emotional, and sensitive nature. CMRs are also able to supplement the data they gather with the greatest degree of their own subjective insight. This was a salient feature of Krieger's research as well, for she could not only hear her respondents talk about their sexual ambivalences, need for reassurances, hopes, and disillusionments, but she could draw on her own firsthand experiences too. She had lived these events and emotions, she was subject to the hopes raised and disillusionments engendered by the community, and she negotiated the ambivalences, uncertainties, and sharply shifting character of the relationships that could be platonic or sexual, both, or neither, on a daily basis. These factors even entered into the dynamics of her interviews.

In other instances, the complete membership role can enable researchers to gain a different perspective on a scene than other researchers could obtain. Thorne's insights into the draft resistance movement, for example, provided her with a view that ultimately differed from both the popular images and from her own, less involved, early impressions. Her initial impression was that the visible group of male leaders was the core of the Resistance. Over time she realized, however, that this social movement, like any institution, depended on the devalued, almost invisible daily labor of subordinates, who were disproportionately women (Thorne, 1983: 234).

CMRs have the further opportunity to acquire "understanding in use" rather than "reconstituted understanding." That is, they can share and grasp the meaning of the members' world as members themselves feel it, as opposed to hearing members recollect and interpret their experiences. During the early phases of Jules-Rosette's research, for example, she found that her respondents spoke about their relation to their religion in one of two vocabularies: "that of the committed believer retrospectively constructing experience and that of perfunctory historical 'fact' " (Jules-Rosette, 1976: 136). To her, these accounts failed to express the phenomenological unfolding of the members' feelings about conversion, belief, and community. After she became baptized, however, she had to learn, for her own pragmatic purposes, a vocabulary of membership to use in interpreting and applying her new found faith in her daily life. After this point her data gathering changed in two primary ways: She gained a deeper, more personal insight into the meaning of church membership for individuals on both the visceral and metaphysical levels, and the conversations she had with members changed because these people could communicate their experiences to her through a vocabulary of understanding they knew she now shared.

Hayano (1982: 155) goes beyond this to argue that achieving complete membership may be the only way to gather some kinds of data:

> Here I have asserted that understanding poker players could not possibly have taken place in any way other than full, complete, long-term submersion, even communion, on the part of the ethnographer. With no formal texts to read, no protracted rituals to witness, and no works of art to admire, there is no other way the multiple layers of facticity, deception, and meanings could properly be interpreted and reconstructed. . . . My attempt to present an insider's view of the work of professional poker players could only be accomplished by prolonged immersion and, most important, *by being a player* [emphasis in original].

Forrest (1986) points out that this is particularly true when researchers are studying worlds hidden from us by the veil of "subjective realities" such as occult or magical settings. These settings are most especially characterized by the existence of multiple or alternate realities and vocabularies of thought. Without entering into these worlds, researchers cannot hope to learn more about them, and the complete membership role is the only mode of entry.

The third consequence of the complete membership role involves its *effects on the researcher's self*. Making a full commitment to membership in a new group, even if this is spurred by research interest, can profoundly alter researchers and their relations with others. Sometimes these effects are just temporary, lasting throughout the research enterprise or for some limited period afterwards. Hayano, for example, became so engrossed in the cardroom world that he withdrew from his family, friends, and job. Pursuing erratic and long hours at the poker tables, often staying up all night, he would arrive at school bleary-eyed and distant. For him the primary locus of reality became the cardrooms where he experienced "powerful personal feelings of frustration and elation." He notes, "By this time I felt more comfortable sitting at a poker table than I did at faculty meetings and in my classes" (Hayano, 1982: 148). These effects began to diminish, however, as he withdrew from the setting. He stopped spending all his free time with his poker buddies and began reintegrating into his family and work. Eventually his life found some new equilibrium, although it was not exactly what it had been before.

When researchers return from the field, they often come back altered by the experience. They may undergo permanent changes in perspective that pertain to some part or the whole of their selves. Thorne, for example, became a feminist as a result of her experiences during the draft resistance movement. Others undergo more far-reaching transformations. Subsequent to her return from the field, Jules-Rosette's conversion continued to retain a profound influence over her. Upon returning to America she felt changed, felt a distance between herself and her friends and colleagues. She describes her difficulty fitting into the place she had left:

> Speaking to old friends was like knocking on an invisible wall. I could not open a box, demonstrate my new faith to them, and then close the box. To speak to them with zeal of my conversion was somehow awkward and impolite [Jules-Rosette, 1976: 163].

As Schutz (1962) notes, neither the homecomer's self nor his home are ever the same once he has departed.

The CMR who made the fullest commitment to membership and who experienced the greatest and most permanent effects, however, was Casteneda. Only he became the true native in the setting, abandoning the social science community and interlinking his future with the other members of his nonordinary reality. The whole of his self became irrevocably altered.

In contrast to the peripheral and active membership roles, there is no role within Gold's (1958) participant observation spectrum that can be easily compared to the complete membership role. This degree of involvement and commitment falls off the end of his spectrum.

The complete member goes beyond the complete participant in several ways. First, the complete member often adopts an overt role. Opportunistic CMRs have little need to pretend to be something they are not, since their values and intentions are aligned with those they study. Convert

CMRs, who are not members when they begin the research, come to the setting with an open and interested (albeit occasionally skeptical) attitude, and undertake a voyage of discovery and membership. While an element of role pretense still remains in the researcher member relationship, it is less than in the other roles. The pretense, separating role and self, comes when CMRs shift between taking the natural stance of the member and the theoretic stance of the researcher. In pursuing their conceptual research goals, they occasionally suppress their natural inclinations for the sake of research relationships and data gathering. There is, however, a great deal more fusion between what Gold calls "self and role," or what Frielich (1970) calls the "human self" and the "research self," than we see in the complete participant. CMRs imbue their role in the field with self-expression and self-integrity.

Perhaps the greatest difference between membership and participation lies in researchers' attitudes toward going native. While complete participants are warned against this occurrence lest they fuse role with self, violate the observer role, and be unable to report their findings, CMRs are urged to embrace the native experience, and to let the member and researcher roles help each other by giving them equal balance and drawing on both. We believe that the native experience does not destroy but, rather, enhances the data-gathering process. Data gathering does not occur *only* through the detached observational role, but through the subjectively immersed role as well.

NOTES

1. While we recognize that controversy surrounds the authenticating and the acceptance of Casteneda's accounts as valid, scholarly sources (DeMille, 1976, 1980), he began his research from a clearly academic perspective and acknowledges his intellectual debt to the anthropologists and sociologists (most especially Garfinkel) with whom he studied (Casteneda, 1968). Moreover, he discusses quite poignantly, through his experiences, the theoretical and methodological issues that are salient to us here. As such, we intend merely to use his work as an archetype of the complete membership role without attesting to the veracity of the self-presentation or analysis. Casteneda's credibility problems raise the issue, on a more general level, of the problem of trust between researchers and readers in all fieldwork. Perhaps the especially tenuous nature of Casteneda's credibility can be traced, in part, to the dual stigma stemming from his huge commercial success and his going native in the field.

2. Davis (1973: 338) has used the term "convert" to refer to the researcher whose "overriding impulse is to immerse himself ever more deeply *within* the frame so that the distinctive subjective currents of the group may forcibly and directly reveal themselves to him." For Davis, this creature is metaphorical and represents no more than one ideal typical pole on the continuum of role closeness versus distance. He advocates that researchers should not be converts, but should balance the closeness of the convert with the distance of the "martian." We, however, treat the convert CMR literally, as an individual moving toward true conversion into the group. Thus, while we use the same term, ours and Davis's meanings differ somewhat.

5. EPILOGUE

Fieldwork is a subjectivist methodology. It employs subjective means to study subjective phenomenon. If we want to get the closest to understanding the human actor in the human world, what Weber (1968) calls the "interpretive undestanding of social action" and what Schutz (1967) calls the "subjective meaning-contexts," we need to channel and marshal our efforts in this direction. To do so we must employ subjectivity, involvement, and commitment.

In a way, this thrust harkens back to the early roots of fieldwork forged by Park and Burgess. They urged people to draw on their own resources, to exploit their backgrounds, in their quest for insight into the subjective character of peoples' lives. This orientation was partly abandoned during the "classical" era, when participant observation replaced the life history approach and the emphasis shifted toward greater objectivity and detachment. Participation was accepted, and accorded legitimacy, but subjectivity, involvement, and commitment were thrust aside. The membership roles method, advocated in this book, draws on the subjectivist orientation of the first generation of Chicagoans, extending it by developing a greater sophistication about the character, nuances, and contours of getting close to the phenomenon one studies.

In the 1980s, the social sciences are in the midst of a renaissance in thinking about subjectivity. Despite the increasing influence of statistical and other "objective" techniques, researchers in education, management, communication, anthropology, and sociology are turning to qualitative approaches with renewed interest. In so doing, they are not always content to follow the dictates of the classical school and bifurcate themselves into two separate parts: the participant, or human, role that interacts with members and forms relationships, and the observer, or research, role that gathers the data. Nor are they always content to subjugate the former in service to the latter.

Actually, we suggest, this distinction has traditionally existed more strongly in theory than in practice; the bifurcation and objectification of self has occurred in the analysis rather than the fieldwork. Most fieldworkers, even those from the classical Chicago School, have followed their social instincts in interacting with members. They knew that the structure of the setting and the personalities of the individuals involved were the most critical determinants of the role the researcher would take, rather than pat scientific rhetoric. They learned from experience, what Douglas (1976) calls their "general cultural understanding" and "general cultural participation," how to feel their way through social encounters and draw on their appropriate human resources in gathering data. In recounting their experiences, though, they cast them into the style of the then current epistemology: that is to say, they suppressed their membership by analyzing their material from the outsider perspective and emphasizing detachment.

We are witness now to the building of a new style of ethnography and epistemology. Fieldworkers have become much more honest and self-reflexive about the extent of their involvement in the settings they study. We have become consciously aware that in order to appreciate the value or evaluate the perspective of each other's work we must know where they stood in the picture and the impact it had on them as well as they on it. We are thus offering profound self-disclosures about very personal aspects of our selves and lives.

We have removed some of the shackles placed upon us by the canons of science and objectivity. We are daring to act in terms of subjectivity, involvement, and commitment. We are allowing ourselves to be honest, not only to ourselves but to our readers. While we have paid "lip service" to Weber's call to subjectivity for over a century, only now are we coming close to developing the methodology implicit in his call for *verstehen*. This represents a modification in fieldwork beyond the one advanced by the second generation of Chicagoans. That is what this book is about.

Throughout the short history of systematic field research, we have grappled with the issues of detachment and objectivity. We realize, more than ever, that while we can never attain the latter, we never risk losing the former. Even the most committed membership-researcher carries detachment into the field. It is embedded, without having to cultivate it, expressly, in each of our unique biographies of multiple roles and inner reflections. To the extent that we accumulate these roles over life into a repertoire, rather than replacing or discarding old ones, we all carry our social science selves into research settings with us. Similarly, we cannot shut out our various other human roles or the feelings generated by these parts of us. The membership roles approach to field research calls on us as researchers to integrate and use our multiple roles in gathering data in the same naturally occuring way we do in our everyday lives. We should not artificially bifurcate ourselves for analytic or scientific elegance. Our goal should be the integration and full use of ourselves as, simultaneously, complex human beings with unique individual biographies and trained and dedicated researchers. To meander through our various roles (to different degrees) over the course of our research is not a grievous error, but a natural human phenomenon. The closer one gets to the phenomenon under study, the more one finds that it dissipates and is, at the same time, continuously re-created by members doing more or less what the membership-researcher is doing. By drawing on our complex and multifaceted human selves (of which the research self is but one dimension, rather than a separate entity), we get closer to the members' behavior.

The membership roles methodology may not be for everyone. Not all settings make membership roles available to researchers, and not all researchers will want to take a membership role in a given setting. Moreover, this is a highly personalistic technique that demands emotionality and intimacy. In both the field and the analysis one has to be revealing; one has to open oneself up and search deep into one's personal characteristics to gain insights, in the way people such as Krieger, Hayano, Peshkin, Rochford, Forrest, and we have done. Membership role research is transformative in character. The researcher *will* be changed by gathering data through this powerfully intensive mode. Therefore *caveat emptor*—let the researcher beware. We believe that the yield more than adequately rewards the cost.

This, then, is what we see as the future of ethnography—people making this kind of commitment and fully immersing themselves in the field; people going beyond participation to membership. We are the research instrument. We acquire more sensitivity, knowledge, and skill each time we delve into another membership world. We must draw on, expand, and continue to dig deeper into our multiple memberships to enlighten the social science community about the worlds in which we live.

REFERENCES

ADLER, P. (1981) Momentum. Newbury Park, CA: Sage.

ADLER, P. (1984) "The sociologist as celebrity: the role of the media in field research." Qualitative Sociology 7: 310-325.

ADLER, P. and P. A. ADLER (1985) "From idealism to pragmatic detachment: the academic performance of college athletes." Sociology of Education 58: 241-250.

ADLER, P. and P. A. ADLER (forthcoming) "The reconstruction of role identity salience: college athletes and the academic role." Social Science Journal.

ADLER, P. A. (1985) Wheeling and Dealing. New York: Columbia University Press.

ADLER, P. A. and P. ADLER (1980) "Symbolic interactionism," pp. 20-61 in J. D. Douglas et al. (eds.) Introduction to the Sociologies of Everyday Life. Boston: Allyn & Bacon.

ALTHEIDE, D. L. (1976) Creating Reality. Newbury Park, CA: Sage.

ANDERSON, N. (1923) The Hobo. Chicago: University of Chicago Press.

ANDERSON, N. (1975) The American Hobo: An Autobiography. Leiden, England: E. J. Brill.

ANDERSON, N. (1983) "A stranger at the gate: reflections on the Chicago School of Sociology." Urban Life 11: 396-406.

BAR-HILLEL, J. (1954) "Indexical expressions." Mind 63: 359-379.

BECKER, H. S. (1963) Outsiders. New York: Free Press.

BECKER, H. S. (1967) "Whose side are we on?" Social Problems 14: 239-247.

BECKER, H. S. and B. GEER (1960) "Participant observation: the analysis of qualitative field data," pp. 267-289 in R. N. Adams and J. J. Preiss (eds.) Human Organization Research: Field Relations and Techniques. Homewood, IL: Dorsey.

BECKER, H. S., B. GEER, and E. HUGHES (1968) Making the Grade. New York: John Wiley.

BECKER, H. S., B. GEER, E. HUGHES, and A. STRAUSS (1961) Boys in White. Chicago: University of Chicago Press.

BELLMAN, B. L. (1984) The Language of Secrecy. New Brunswick, NJ: Rutgers University Press.

BITTNER, E. (1967) "The police on skid row: a study of peace keeping." American Sociological Review 32: 699-715.

BITTNER, E. (1973) "Objectivity and realism in sociology," pp. 109-125 in G. Psathas (ed.) Phenomenological Sociology. New York: John Wiley.

BLUMER, H. (1962) "Society as symbolic interaction," pp. 179-192 in A. Rose (ed.) Human Behavior and Social Processes. Boston: Houghton Mifflin.

BLUMER, H. (1969) Symbolic Interaction. Englewood Cliffs, NJ: Prentice-Hall.

BOGDAN, R. and S. J. TAYLOR (1975) Introduction to Qualitative Research Methods. New York: John Wiley.

BRUYN, S. T. (1966) The Human Perspective in Sociology: The Methodology of Participant Observation. Englewood Cliffs, NJ: Prentice-Hall.

BULMER, M. (1980) "Comment on the ethics of covert research." British Journal of Sociology 31: 59-65.

BULMER, M. (1983) "The methodology of the Taxi-Dance Hall." Urban Life 12: 95-101.

BULMER, M. (1984) The Chicago School of Sociology. Chicago: University of Chicago Press.

BURGESS, E. W. (1927) "Statistics and case studies as methods of sociological research." Sociology and Social Research 12: 103-120.

BURGESS, R. G. (1982) "Some role problems in field research," pp. 45-49 in R. G. Burgess (ed.) Field Research: A Sourcebook and Field Manual. London: George Allen & Unwin.

CAREY, J. T. (1972) "Problems of access and risk in observing drug scenes," pp. 71-92 in J. D. Douglas (ed.) Research on Deviance. New York: Random House.

CASSELL, J. (1980) "Ethical principles for conducting fieldwork." American Anthropologist 82: 28-41.

CASSELL, J. and M. WAX (1980) "Toward a moral science of human beings." Social Problems 27: 259-264.

CASTENEDA, C. (1968) The Teachings of Don Juan. New York: Ballentine.

CASTENEDA, C. (1971) A Separate Reality. New York: Simon & Schuster.

CASTENEDA, C. (1972) Journey to Ixtlan. New York: Washington Square Press.

CASTENEDA, C. (1974) Tales of Power. New York: Simon & Schuster.

CASTENEDA, C. (1977) The Second Ring of Power. New York: Simon & Schuster.

CASTENEDA, C. (1981) The Eagle's Gift. New York: Simon & Schuster.

CASTENEDA, C. (1984) The Fire from Within. New York: Pocket.

CAVAN, R. S. (1983) "The Chicago School of Sociology, 1918-1933." Urban Life 11: 407-420.

CAVAN, S. (1972) Hippies of the Haight. St. Louis: New Critics Press.

CICOUREL, A. (1964) Method and Measurement in Sociology. New York: Free Press.

CICOUREL, A. (1974a) Theory and Method in a Study of Argentine Fertility. New York: John Wiley.

CICOUREL, A. (1974b) Cognitive Sociology. New York: Free Press.

CORSINO, L. (1984) "Underinvolvement and the dynamics of personality: notes on bias in field research situations." Unpublished manuscript. (Adapted from "The making of a campaign organization," doctoral dissertation, University of Massachusetts, Amherst, 1978.)

CRESSEY, P. G. (1932) The Taxi Dance Hall. Chicago: University of Chicago Press.

CRESSEY, P. G. (1983) "A comparison of the roles of the 'sociological stranger' and the 'anonymous stranger' in field research." Urban Life 12: 102-120.

CUFF, E. C. and G.C.F. PAYNE (1984) Perspectives in Sociology (2nd. ed.). London: George Allen & Unwin.

CUMMINS, M. et al. (1972) Report of the Student Task Force on Heroin Use in Metropolitan Saint Louis. Saint Louis: Washington University Social Science Institute.

DAVIS, F. (1963) Passage Through Crisis. Indianapolis: Bobbs-Merrill.

DAVIS, F. (1973) "The martian and the convert: ontological polarities in social research." Urban Life 2: 333-343.

DAVIS, F. (1986) Personal communication.

DeMILLE, R. (1976) Casteneda's Journey. Santa Barbara, CA: Capra Press.

DeMILLE, R. [ed.] (1980) The Don Juan Papers. Santa Barbara, CA: Ross-Erikson.

DENZIN, N. K. (1970) The Research Act. Chicago: Aldine.

DOUGLAS, J. D. (1970) "Understanding everyday life," pp. 3-44 in J. D. Douglas (ed.) Understanding Everyday Life. Chicago: Aldine.

DOUGLAS, J. D. (1972) "Observing deviance," pp. 3-34 in J. D. Douglas (ed.) Research on Deviance. New York: Random House.

DOUGLAS, J. D. (1976) Investigative Social Research. Newbury Park, CA: Sage.

DOUGLAS, J. D. (1985) Creative Interviewing. Newbury Park, CA: Sage.

DOUGLAS, J. D. and J. M. JOHNSON [eds.] (1977) Existential Sociology. New York: Cambridge University Press.

DOUGLAS, J. D. and P. K. RASMUSSEN (1977) The Nude Beach. Newbury Park, CA: Sage.

EASTERDAY, L., D. PAPADEMAS, L. SCHORR, and C. VALENTINE (1977) "The making of a female researcher: role problems in field work." Urban Life 6: 333-348.

EMERSON, R. M. (1983) "Introduction," pp. 1-35 in R. M. Emerson (ed.) Contemporary Field Research. Boston: Little, Brown.

ERIKSON, K. T. (1967) "A comment on disguised observation in sociology." Social Problems 12: 366-373.

EVANS-PRITCHARD, E. E. (1973) "Some reminiscences and reflections on fieldwork." Journal of the Anthropological Society of Oxford 4: 1-12.

EVERHART, R. B. (1977) "Between stranger and friend: some consequences of 'long term' fieldwork in schools." American Education Research Journal 14: 1-15.

FAUGHT, J. (1980) "Presuppositions of the Chicago School in the work of Everett C. Hughes." The American Sociologist 15: 72-82.

FEYERABEND, P. F. (1972) Against Method. London: New Left Books.

FONTANA, A. (1980) "Toward a complex universe: existential sociology," pp. 155-181 in J. D. Douglas et al. (eds.) Introduction to the Sociologies of Everyday Life. Boston: Allyn & Bacon.

FORREST, B. (1986) "Apprentice-participation: methodology and the study of subjective reality." Urban Life 14: 431-453.

FORREST, B. (forthcoming) "Hello central, get me heaven." Doctoral dissertation, University of California, San Diego.

FREEMAN, C. R. (1980) "Phenomenological sociology and ethnomethodology," pp. 113-153 in J. D. Douglas et al. (eds.) Introduction to the Sociologies of Everyday Life. Boston: Allyn & Bacon.

FREILICH, M. (1970) "Toward a formalization of field work," pp. 485-585 in M. Freilich (ed.) Marginal Natives. New York: Harper & Row.

GANS, H. J. (1982a) The Urban Villagers (2nd. ed.). New York: Free Press.

GANS, H. J. (1982b) "The participant observer as a human being: observations on the personal aspects of fieldwork," pp. 53-61 in R. G. Burgess (ed.) Field Research: A Sourcebook and Field Manual. London: George Allen and Unwin.

GANS, H. J. (1985) Personal communication.

GARFINKEL, H. (1952) "The perception of the other: a study in social order." Doctoral dissertation, Harvard University.

GARFINKEL, H. (1967) Studies in Ethnomethodology. Englewood Cliff, NJ: Prentice-Hall.

GARFINKEL, H. (1980) Class notes. University of California, Los Angeles.

GARFINKEL, H. and H. SACKS (1970) "On formal structures of practical activities," pp. 338-366 in E. Tiryakian and J. McKinney (eds.) Theoretical Sociology. New York: Appleton-Century-Croft.

GARFINKEL, H., M. LYNCH, and E. LIVINGSTON (1981) "The work of a discovering science construed with materials from the optically discovered pulsar." Philosophy of Social Science 11: 131-158.

GEERTZ, C. (1973) The Interpretation of Cultures: Selected Essays. New York: Basic Books.

GOFFMAN, E. (1959) The Presentation of Self in Everyday Life. Garden City, NY: Doubleday.

GOLD, R. L. (1950) "The Chicago Flat Janitor." Master's thesis, University of Chicago.

GOLD, R. L. (1958) "Roles in sociological field observations." Social Forces 36: 217-223.

GOLDE, P. [ed.] (1970) Women in the Field. Chicago: Aldine.

GUSFIELD, J. (1963) Symbolic Crusade. Urbana: University of Illinois Press.

HABENSTEIN, R. (1954) The American Funeral Director. Doctoral dissertation, University of Chicago.

HAMMERSLEY, M. and P. ATKINSON (1983) Ethnography: Principles in Practice. New York: Tavistock.

HANDEL, W. H. (1982) Ethnomethodology. Englewood Cliffs, NJ: Prentice-Hall.

HAYANO, D. M. (1979) "Auto-ethnography: paradigms, problems, and prospects." Human Organization 38: 99-104.

HAYANO, D. M. (1982) Poker Faces. Berkeley: University of California Press.

HERITAGE, J. (1984) Garfinkel and Ethnomethodology. Cambridge, England: Polity.

HIGGINS, P. (1980) Outsiders in a Hearing World. Newbury Park, CA: Sage.

HOFFMAN, J. E. (1980) "Problems of access in the study of social elites and boards of directors," pp. 45-56 in W. B. Shaffir, R. A. Stebbins, and A. Turowetz (eds.) Fieldwork Experience. New York: St. Martin's.

HOROWITZ, R. (1983) Honor and The American Dream. New Brunswick, NJ: Rutgers University Press.

HOROWITZ, R. (1986) "Remaining an outsider: membership as a threat to research rapport." Urban Life 14: 409-430.

HOSTETLER, J. A. (1968) Amish Society. Baltimore: Johns Hopkins University Press.

HUGHES, E. C. (1945) "Dilemmas and contradictions of status." American Journal of Sociology 50: 353-359.

HUGHES, E. C. (1971) The Sociological Eye. Chicago: Aldine.

HUNT, J. (1984) "The development of rapport through the negotiation of gender in field work among police." Human Organization 43: 283-296.

HUNT, J. (1985) Personal communication.

HUSSERL, E. (1962) Ideal: General Introduction to Pure Phenomenology. New York: Collier.

HUSSERL, E. (1965) Phenomenology and the Crisis of Philosophy. New York: Harper & Row.

HUSSERL, E. (1969) Formal and Transcendental Logic. The Hague: Martinus Nijhoff.

HUSSERL, E. (1970) Cartesian Meditations. The Hague: Martinus Nijhoff.

JAMES, W. (1890) Principles of Psychology (2 vols.). New York: Henry Holt.

JANES, R. W. (1961) "A note on the phases of the community role of the participant observer." American Sociological Review 26: 446-450.

JARVIE, I. C. (1969) "The problem of ethical integrity in participant observation." Current Anthropology 10: 505-508.

JOHNSON, J. M. (1975) Doing Field Research. New York: Free Press.

JULES-ROSETTE, B. (1975) African Apostles. Ithaca, NY: Cornell University Press.

JULES-ROSETTE, B. (1976) "The conversion experience: the apostles of John Maranke." Journal of Religion in Africa 7: 132-164.

JUNKER, B. H. (1960) Field Work: An Introduction to the Social Sciences. Chicago: University of Chicago Press.

KAUFFMAN, F. (1944) Methodology of the Social Sciences. New York: Humanities.

KIRBY, R. and J. CORZINE (1981) "The contagion of stigma." Qualitative Sociology 4: 3-20.

KOTARBA, J. A. (1983) Chronic Pain. Newbury Park, CA: Sage.

KRIEGER, S. (1983) The Mirror Dance: Identity in a Women's Community. Philadelphia: Temple University Press.

KRIEGER, S. (1985) "Beyond 'subjectivity': the use of the self in social science." Qualitative Sociology 8: 309-324.

LANDESCO, J. (1925) "The criminal gang," in Reports to the LCRC, autumn quarter.

LANDESCO, J. (1929) Organized Crime in Chicago. Chicago: Illinois Association for Criminal Justice.

LEITER, K. (1980) A Primer on Ethnomethodology. New York: Oxford University Press.

LeMASTERS, E. E. (1975) Blue-Collar Aristocrats. Madison: University of Wisconsin Press.

LIEBOW, E. (1967) Tally's Corner. Boston: Little, Brown.

LOFLAND, J. (1966) Doomsday Cult. Englewood Cliffs, NJ: Prentice-Hall.

LOFLAND, J. (1971) Analyzing Social Settings. Belmont, CA: Wadsworth.

LOFLAND, J. (1976) Doing Social Life. New York: John Wiley.

LOFLAND, J. and R. STARK (1965) "Becoming a world-saver: a theory of conversion to a deviant perspective." American Sociological Review 30: 862-875.

MACHIAVELLI, N. (1970) The Prince. New York: Washington Square Press.

MANNHEIM, K. (1952) Essays on the Sociology of Knowledge. London: Routledge & Kegan Paul.

MARQUART, J. W. (1983) "Cooptation of the kept: maintaining control in a southern penitentiary." Doctoral dissertation, Texas A&M University.

MARQUART, J. W. (1985) "Doing research in prison: the strengths and weaknesses of full participation as a guard." Unpublished manuscript, Mississippi State University. (Published in a revised form in Justice Quarterly, 1986, 3: 15-32.)

MAYNARD, D. (1986) "New treatment for an old itch." Contemporary Sociology 15: 346-349.

McCALL, G. J. and J. L. SIMMONS [eds.] (1969) Issues in Participant Observation. Reading, MA: Addison Wesley.

MEHAN, H. and H. WOOD (1975) The Reality of Ethnomethodology. New York: John Wiley.

MILLER, S. M. (1952) "The participant observer and 'over-rapport.'" American Sociological Review 17: 97-99.

MITCHELL, R. (1983) Mountain Experience. Chicago: University of Chicago Press.

OLESON, V. and E. WHITTAKER (1967) "Role-making in participant observation: processes in the researcher-actor relationship." Human Organization 26: 273-281.

PALMER, V. (1928) Field Studies in Sociology. Chicago: University of Chicago Press.

PARK, R. E. (1915) "The city: suggestions for the investigation of human behavior in the urban environment." American Journal of Sociology 20: 577-612.

PARK, R. E. (1929) "The city as a social laboratory," in T. V. Smith and L. D. White (eds.) Chicago: An Experiment in Social Science Research. Chicago: University of Chicago Press.

PARK, R. E. (1950) Race and Culture. Glencoe, IL: Free Press.

PARK, R. E. (1973) "Life history." American Journal of Sociology 79: 251-260.

PAUL, B. D. (1953) "Interview techniques and field relationships," pp. 430-451 in A. L. Kroeber (ed.) Anthropology Today. Chicago: University of Chicago Press.

PESHKIN, A. (1984) "Odd man out: the participant observer in an absolutist setting." Sociology of Education 57: 254-264.

PESHKIN, A. (1985) "Virtuous subjectivity: in the participant-observer's I's," pp. 267-281 in D. N. Berg and K. K. Smith (eds.) Exploring Clinical Methods for Social Research. Newbury Park, CA: Sage.

PESHKIN, A. (1986) God's Choice. Chicago: University of Chicago Press.

PHILLIPS, D. (1974) "Epistemology and the sociology of knowledge." Theory and Society 1: 59-88.

PLATT, J. (1981) "Whatever happened to the case study? Or from Znaniecki to Lazarsfeld in one generation." Unpublished manuscript, University of Sussex.

PLATT, J. (1983) "The development of the 'participant observation' method in sociology: origin, myth, and history." Journal of the History of the Behavioral Sciences 19: 379-393.

POLLNER, M. (1970) "On the foundations of mundane reason." Doctoral dissertation, University of California, Santa Barbara.

POLLNER, M. and R. M. EMERSON (1983) "The dynamics of inclusion and distance in fieldwork relations," pp. 235-252 in R. M. Emerson (ed.) Contemporary Field Research. Boston: Little, Brown.

POLSKY, N. (1969) Hustlers, Beats, and Others. Garden City, NY: Anchor.

PONSE, B. (1976) "Secrecy in the lesbian world." Urban Life 5: 313-338.

POWDERMAKER, H. (1966) Stranger and Friend: The Way of an Anthropologist. New York: Norton.

PRUS, R. C. and C.R.D. SHARPER (1977) Road Hustler. Lexington, MA: D. C. Heath.

RADCLIFFE-BROWN, A. R. (1958) "The method of ethnology and social anthropology," in M. N. Srinivas (ed.) Method in Social Anthropology. Chicago: University of Chicago Press.

REIMAN, J. H. (1979) "Research subjects, political subjects, and human subjects," pp. 35-57 in C. B. Klockars and F. W. O'Conner (eds.) Deviance and Decency. Newbury Park, CA: Sage.

REINHARZ, S. (1979) On Becoming a Social Scientist: From Survey Research and Participation to Experiential Analysis. San Francisco: Jossey-Bass.

RIEMER, J. W. (1977) "Varieties of opportunistic research." Urban Life 5: 467-477.

RIESMAN, D. (1983) "The legacy of Everett Hughes." Contemporary Sociology 12: 477-481.

ROCHFORD, E. B., Jr. (1983) "Stutterers' practices: folk remedies and therapeutic intervention." Journal of Communication Disorders 16: 373-384.

ROCHFORD, E. B., Jr. (1985) Hare Krishna in America. New Brunswick, NJ: Rutgers University Press.

ROCK, P. (1979) The Making of Symbolic Interactionism. Totowa, NJ: Rowman & Littlefield.

ROTH, J. (1963) Timetables. Indianapolis: Bobbs-Merrill.

SCHATZMAN, L. and A. L. STRAUSS (1973) Field Research: Strategies for a Natural Sociology. Englewood Cliffs, NJ: Prentice-Hall.

SCHEGLOFF, E. and H. SACKS (1974) "Opening up closings," pp. 233-264 in R. Turner (ed.) Ethnomethodology. Baltimore: Penguin.

SCHUTZ, A. (1962) Collected Papers I: The Problem of Social Reality (ed. by M. Natanson). The Hague: Martinus Nijhoff.

SCHUTZ, A. (1964) Collected Papers II: Studies in Social Theory (ed. by M. Natanson). The Hague: Martinus Nijhoff.

SCHUTZ, A. (1966) Collected Papers III: Studies in Phenomenological Philosophy (ed. by M. Natanson). The Hague: Martinus Nijhoff.

SCHUTZ, A. (1967) The Phenomenology of the Social World. Evanston, IL: Northwestern University Press.

SCHWARTZ, H. and J. JACOBS (1979) Qualitative Sociology. New York: Free Press.

SCHWARTZ, M. S. and C. G. SCHWARTZ (1955) "Problems in participant observation." American Journal of Sociology 60: 343-353.

SCOTT, M. (1968) The Racing Game. Chicago: Aldine.

SHALIN, D. N. (1986) "Pragmatism and social interactionism." American Sociological Review 51: 9-29.

SPRADLEY, J. P. (1980) Participant Observation. New York: Holt, Rinehart & Winston.

SNOW, D. A. (1980) "The disengagement process: a neglected problem in participant observation research." Qualitative Sociology 3: 100-122.

STEIN, M. R. (1964) "The eclipse of community: some glances at the education of a sociologist," pp. 207-232 in A. J. Vidich, J. Bensman, and M. R. Stein (eds.) Reflections on Community Studies. New York: Harper & Row.

STONE, G. S. (1959) "Clothing and social relations." Doctoral dissertation, University of Chicago.

SUDNOW, D. [ed.] (1972) Studies in Social Interaction. New York: Free Press.

SUDNOW, D. (1978) Ways of the Hand. New York: Harper & Row.

THOMAS, J. (1983a) "Toward a critical ethnography." Urban Life 11: 477-490.

THOMAS, J. (1983b) "Chicago sociology: an introduction." Urban Life 11: 387-395.

THOMAS, W. I. and F. ZNANIECKI (1923) The Polish Peasant in Europe and America. Chicago: University of Chicago Press.

THORNE, B. (1971) "Resisting the draft: an ethnography of the draft resistance movement." Doctoral dissertation, Brandeis University.

THORNE, B. (1983) "Political activist as participant observer: conflicts of commitment in a study of the draft resistance movement in the 1960s," pp. 216-234 in R. M. Emerson (ed.) Contemporary Field Research. Boston: Little, Brown.

THRASHER, F. M. (1927) The Gang. Chicago: University of Chicago Press.

THRASHER, F. M. (1982) "How to study the boys' gang in the open." Journal of Educational Sociology 1: 244-254.

TRICE, H. M. (1956) "The 'outsider's' role in field study." Sociology and Social Research 41: 27-32.

VIDICH, A. J. (1955) "Participant observation and the collection and interpretation of data." American Journal of Sociology 60: 354-360.

WARNER, W. L. and P. S. LUNT (1941) The Social Life of a Modern Community. New Haven, CT: Yale University Press.

WARNER, W. L. and P. S. LUNT (1942) The Status System of a Modern Community. New Haven, CT: Yale University Press.

WARREN, C.A.B. and P. K. RASMUSSEN (1977) "Sex and gender in field research." Urban Life 6: 349-369.

WARWICK, D. P. (1974) "Who deserves protection?" American Sociologist 9: 158-159.

WAX, M. (1986) Personal communication.

WAX, R. H. (1952) "Reciprocity as a field technique." Human Organization 11: 34-37.

WAX, R. H. (1971) Doing Fieldwork. Chicago: University of Chicago Press.

WAX, R. H. (1979) "Gender and age in fieldwork and fieldwork education: no good thing is done by any man alone." Social Problems 26: 509-522.

WEBER, M. (1949) The Methodology of the Social Sciences. New York: Free Press.

WEBER, M. (1968) Economy and Society. New York: Bedminster.

WEIDER, D. L. (1974) Language and Social Reality: The Case of Telling the Convict. The Hague: Mouton.

WHYTE, W. F. (1955) Street Corner Society. Chicago: University of Chicago Press.

WILLIAMS, T. R. (1967) Field Methods in the Study of Culture. New York: Holt, Rinehart & Winston.

WILLIS, P. (1977) Learning to Labour: How Working Class Kids Get Working Class Jobs. New York: Columbia University Press.

ZIMMERMAN, D. H. (1970) "The practicalities of rule use," pp. 221-238 in J. D. Douglas (ed.) Understanding Everyday Life. Chicago: Aldine.

ZURCHER, L. A. (1977) The Mutable Self. Newbury Park, CA: Sage.

ABOUT THE AUTHORS

PATRICIA A. ADLER and PETER ADLER received their A.B.s from Washington University, St. Louis, M.A.s from the University of Chicago, and Ph.D.s from the University of California, San Diego. His book, *Momentum*, was published by Sage in 1981 and her book, *Wheeling and Dealing*, was published by Columbia University Press in 1985. They are also coauthors of *Introduction to the Sociologies of Everyday Life* (Allyn & Bacon, 1980). In addition to editing *The Social Dynamics of Financial Markets* (JAI Press, 1984) and the research annual, *Sociological Studies of Child Development*, they have served as Associate Editors of *Social Problems* and *Qualitative Sociology*. They are currently the editors of the *Journal of Contemporary Ethnography* (formerly *Urban Life*).They have published widely in the areas of qualitative methodology, social psychology, sociology of sport, sociology of education, sociology of childhood, and deviant behavior. Currently, he is Associate Professor and Chair of the Department of Sociology at the University of Denver, and she is Assistant Professor in the Department of Sociology at the University of Colorado, Boulder.

NOTES

DATE DUE